THE GET
HEALTHY
GO VEGAN
COOKBOOK

THE GET HEALTHY
HEALTHY
GO VEGAN
COOKBOOK

Neal Barnard, MD,
and **Robyn Webb**

DA CAPO LIFELONG
A MEMBER OF THE PERSEUS BOOKS GROUP

The Get Healthy, Go Vegan Cookbook. Copyright © 2010
by Neal Barnard, MD, and Robyn Webb
Photography by Firefly Photography

Design and production by Neuwirth & Associates
Cataloging-in-Publication data for this book is available from the Library of Congress.
First Da Capo Press edition 2010
ISBN: 978-0-7382-1358-3

Published by Da Capo Press
A Member of the Perseus Books Group
www.dacapopress.com

Note: This book is intended only as an informative guide for those wishing to know more about health issues. In no way is this book intended to replace, countermand, or conflict with the advice given to you by your own physician. The ultimate decision concerning care should be made between you and your doctor. We strongly recommend you follow his or her advice. Information in this book is general and is offered with no guarantees on the part of the authors or Da Capo Press. The authors and publisher disclaim all liability in connection with the use of this book.

Da Capo Press books are available at special discounts for bulk purchases in the U.S. by corporations, institutions, and other organizations. For more information, please contact the Special Markets Department at the Perseus Books Group, 2300 Chestnut Street, Suite 200, Philadelphia, PA, 19103, or call (800) 810-4145, ext. 5000, or e-mail special.markets@perseusbooks.com.

10 9 8 7 6 5 4

CONTENTS

INTRODUCTION

THIS BOOK HOLDS the culinary secrets to lifelong health. These 125 easy and delicious recipes will lure you with their aromas and flavors, many familiar, some new. But what awaits you is more than simply a treat for the taste buds. These recipes are powerful. They will help you trim down, lower your cholesterol, bring your blood sugar and blood pressure under control, and get your energy back. And if you are healthy now, these wonderful foods will help you stay that way.

As it stands, most people are not eating very well. In North America, our dietary staples are not vegetables, fruits, brown rice, or other healthful foods. No, for many people, a meal is not a meal unless there is a big chunk of meat in the middle of the plate, with a little pile of green beans or corn tossed in as an after-thought. That was the way it was when I grew up, and I suspect something similar may have been true for you, too.

As a result of our less-than-healthful eating habits, Americans tend to be heavier than people from other countries, and, perhaps surprisingly, we do not live as long as they do. Even with our high-tech medical care, Americans are likely to be felled by heart attacks, cancer, diabetes, or other problems. Our lives are about four years shorter on average compared with that of people in Japan, where the dietary staples are reversed: rice, noodles, and vegetables are mainstays, while meat traditionally serves mainly as a flavoring. And our quality of life suffers, too. We are less able to work, dance, or play tennis in our later years, and are more likely to be on medicines or in the hospital.

And things are worsening year by year. Back in the 1960s, bacon and eggs showed up at breakfast, and roast beef and gravy were on America's dinner plates. Lunch may or may not have been another meaty meal. And then McDonald's arrived, as did Burger King, Wendy's, and Pizza Hut. They were not selling broccoli, carrots, and asparagus sushi. Even in the smallest cities, these fast-food restaurants ushered in a load of meat, cheese, and soda that pushed fat and calories to unprecedented levels in our diets. Here are the numbers:

▶ When the federal government began keeping records in 1909, the average American ate about 124 pounds of meat per year. By 1970, that figure had soared to over 175 pounds. As the new millennium arrived, the figure burst through the 200-pound mark.
▶ A century ago, the average American ate less than 4 pounds of cheese in an entire year. By 2009, that figure was over 33 pounds, thanks to cheeseburgers, cheese pizza, and cheese on just about everything else.
▶ Sugar intake has risen by about 20 pounds per person per year just since 1970.

In other words, our eating habits were never very good in North America, but in recent decades they have gotten a whole lot worse. An ever-increasing load of meat, cheese, and sugar makes weight problems inevitable. Today, two-thirds of Americans are beyond the boundaries of a healthy weight, and American children are in the worst shape of any generation in history.

The results are not just apparent on the bathroom scale. They also show up in unprecedented numbers of people lined up in pharmacies to buy diet aids, insulin, cholesterol-lowering drugs, and blood-pressure medicines.

And the problem is not limited to North America. India, China, and much of the rest of the world, where healthy grains and vegetables have historically played major roles, now follow America's lead, loading up on burgers and pizza. And as Western dietary habits spread worldwide, Western diseases like cancer and diabetes follow along.

The answer is to take advantage of the foods our bodies are designed for. Vegetables and fruits provide beta-carotene and lycopene to help shore up our bodies' defenses against cancer, along with thousands of other nutrients with health power that cannot be matched by meat-based diets. Whole grains and beans are loaded with fiber to help trim our waistlines and cut cholesterol, not to mention plenty of protein, iron, and calcium. By setting aside animal-derived products—meat, dairy products, and eggs—you can reach a level of health and well-being that you may never have expected you could enjoy.

At the Physicians Committee for Responsible Medicine in Washington, D.C., we conduct research projects to study how foods affect health. We also sponsor educational programs to help people change their eating habits and improve their health. Some of the people who participate in our programs simply want to expand their repertoire of healthful foods. Others have a few pounds they'd like to lose. Many have a lot of pounds to lose, not to mention fairly serious health problems that they really *have* to conquer.

And yet so many people do not know about the power of healthful eating. That's why we wrote this book. We want to help people understand how fueling the body with the right foods can lead to an enormous health payoff. We aim to provide a menu that is as close to perfect as humanly possible. And we hope to show how easy it is to prepare truly healthful foods and what a delight it can be to serve them to family and friends.

I am a physician. After completing medical school and residency at the George Washington University in Washington, D.C., I began my professional life as a psychiatrist, helping people overcome serious behavioral problems. Later, I had a major career change. Having led several research studies on diet and health, I am now an adjunct associate professor of medicine in the Department of Internal Medicine at the George Washington University School of Medicine. I also head the Physicians Committee for Responsible Medicine, which promotes healthful diets and conducts research, as I mentioned above, and also promotes ethical research, pushes for improved food policies, and hosts many information-packed Web sites that I hope you will visit.

My coauthor, Robyn, is a culinary wizard who has healthful cooking in her blood. Growing up in the food business, she knows how to turn simple, healthful ingredients into knockout meals. In our research work, she shows even the most timid person that the kitchen counter is a place where magical things can happen.

Although our work has focused on helping people trim down, conquer diabetes, cut cholesterol, and tackle other medical problems, it should be said that not everyone who decides to forgo animal products makes that choice for health reasons. Many people are concerned with how animals are treated by the food industries, and rightly so. And the environmental consequences of meat and dairy production should be of concern to all of us. Whatever your reason for looking at a new direction, we hope you enjoy this treasury of healthful, delicious recipes.

A Word about Language

Words about food can be confusing. Just so we're all on the same page, let's define a few:

- ▶ An omnivorous diet includes anything and everything.
- ▶ A vegetarian diet excludes meat, although some people hedge on whether fish or chicken count as meat.
- ▶ A vegan (vee´ gun) diet is one type of vegetarian diet. By definition, it excludes anything from animal sources—meat, dairy products, eggs, and even honey.

Following a vegan diet does not necessarily mean that a person is making choices for moral reasons and does not mean that he or she avoids using animal-derived products, such as leather or fur, although many people soon come to recognize that there are ethical issues any time animals are used.

Also, I suggest using these words mainly as adjectives, not nouns (that is, I will usually speak of "a vegan diet," rather than referring to people as "vegans"), which is a good practice anytime we are speaking of choices and beliefs. The idea is that we can change. A man following an omnivorous diet who switches to a vegan diet is still the same guy he always was. His character has not changed at all. The only thing different is what is on his plate. But to say that he was once "an omnivore" and is now "a vegan" can conjure up all sorts of images about politics, tastes, and lifestyle that may not apply.

This adjective-versus-noun rule is not hard and fast, even in this book. But it is one you'll find useful, and not just for food choices. Think about how words like "diabetic," "liberal," "conservative," "atheist," "socialist," "disabled," and many others evoke images when used as nouns.

Please page through this book at your own pace, put its treasures to work, and, above all, share it with others. It is a joy to help people eat more sensibly, and we are delighted to have you help us spread the word.

NEAL D. BARNARD, MD

THE GET
HEALTHY
GO VEGAN
COOKBOOK

GET
HEALTHY!
PART
1

REVOLUTIONIZE YOUR MENU, REVOLUTIONIZE YOUR LIFE

BETHESDA, MARYLAND, IS ground zero for medical research. On the outskirts of Washington, D.C., Bethesda is the home of the National Institutes of Health (NIH), where billions upon billions of dollars are dedicated to searching for answers to life-threatening problems. NIH researchers work with sophisticated scanning devices, radioactive isotopes, and all manner of novel chemicals, hoping to build ever-more-powerful bullets to attack killer diseases.

But in 2003, NIH funded a team of researchers to test a completely different strategy. The problem was diabetes, a disease affecting 200 million people worldwide, often shortening their lives and causing disabling complications. Diabetes treatment is certainly high tech, with a continual stream of new medications and very sophisticated methods for tracking how the condition affects the human body. But instead of aiming to develop a new and better drug to manage diabetes, NIH funded a research team—our team—to attack its *cause,* and our "medicine" was food.

Our research is conducted at the offices of the Physicians Committee for Responsible Medicine, an organization I founded in 1985 bring a new emphasis to prevention, nutrition, and ethical research. Our staffers have taught thousands of people how foods can help heart disease, cancer, and other serious problems, not to mention such annoyances as arthritis pain and headaches. In the early 1990s, we began a series of research studies to find new and better ways to prevent and manage health problems.

In 2003 we set our sights on using food to reverse diabetes. We brought in ninety-nine people with type 2 diabetes, taught them how to improve their diets, and tracked how they did for a year and a half.

People volunteering for the study certainly needed help. Many had lost family members to the disease and had seen how it can cause blindness, loss of limbs, and loss of kidney function.

Many of our research participants also had high blood pressure, high cholesterol, and quite a bit of weight they wanted to lose. Nearly all were on medication, and most had come to feel there was no way they could regain their health.

The nutritional approach we chose had three parts. We avoided animal products, kept oils to a minimum, and avoided sugary, processed foods. As our study began, we already had an inkling a plant-based diet would help these conditions. Not only had our preliminary studies been very promising; other researchers had shown that nutrition, when properly applied, can be an enormously powerful force.

For example, Dr. Dean Ornish had shown that, with the right diet and lifestyle changes, coronary arteries, blocked by years of unhealthful foods, can actually open up again, dramatically reducing the risk of heart attacks. Other researchers had shown that similar changes powerfully lower cholesterol and blood pressure. So we were very pleased, but not surprised, to find that our diabetes study patients thrived with vegan foods. They lost weight. Many reduced or even eliminated their use of medications, and felt better than they had in years.

They also came to view foods very differently. After all, we did not simply reduce meat in their diets and boost their veggies a bit. We cut the meats out completely. We cut out dairy products and eggs, too. And we really emphasized the healthiest foods— vegetables, fruits, whole grains, and beans.

When you take these steps, good things happen in your body. Your cholesterol level plummets, allowing your arteries to recover from years of abuse. Hormones within your body rebalance, bringing your blood sugar to a healthier level, trimming away excess weight, and reducing cancer risk. Your digestion improves, and your energy increases.

But the reason this approach is so successful is not simply that these foods are powerful. They are also so delicious and easy to prepare, you would not want to go back to your old way of eating. In other words, this is not a "diet" that you turn on when you need it and abandon a few weeks later. Rather, it is a whole new way of thinking about foods—a way of using foods to nourish and heal your body. It is as natural as breathing, and once you have experienced how good you can feel, sticking with it is more or less automatic.

I Can Do It!

That's right, you can! We hear these words again and again from people who had thought their health was slipping away. After years of weight gain, ever-worsening laboratory tests, and more and more prescriptions, many people feel that things simply cannot get better.

But, when you put the power of healthful nutrition to work, the effects can be astounding.

▶ Vance had been a Washington, D.C., policeman for twelve years. His father had passed away at the age of thirty. And Vance was just thirty-one when he was diagnosed with diabetes. He had had it for five years before joining our research study, by which time his blood sugar was completely out of control. Vance told me how his diet had included barbecued meat, chicken wings, and other less-than-healthy foods. With our help, he got started on a better path. To his surprise, it turned out to be easy, and the effects were amazing. Weight melted away—60 pounds over the next year. His blood sugar gradually came down to the normal range. And eventually his doctor—amazed by Vance's progress—told him the magic words: it was time to stop his diabetes medications. He didn't need them anymore.

▶ Ashley started gaining weight in college, and carried about 30 extra pounds through her twenties. After her first child was born, her weight ratcheted up a bit more. Both of her parents had gained considerable weight in midlife, so she assumed that the problem was probably genetic—and inevitable. Then, during a medical appointment, the nurse called the doctor into the room urgently. The nurse had been taking Ashley's blood pressure, which turned out to be dangerously high. The doctor walked her to the emergency room himself, and had her admitted to the hospital overnight.

Fast-forward ten years. After a decade of continual weight gain and an ever-increasing regimen of blood pressure medications, Ashley happened to hear a radio program in which I described our nutritional approach. She gave it a try. The first week was easy enough, and she lost two or three pounds, and her blood pressure started to descend, seemingly on its own. She trimmed away 35 pounds in the first six months and 20 more in the next six months. Today, she fits into her college jeans, is off all medications, and has the blood pressure of a teenager.

▶ Selwyn had had diabetes for almost twenty years when he came to our center. Even with three insulin injections per day, his complications were gradually worsening. The disease had attacked his eyes, necessitating laser treatments. Even worse was the pain in his feet—a condition called diabetic neuropathy, for which there is no good and reliable treatment.

But Selwyn jumped into a new approach to eating. Even without adding any exercise, his blood sugar improved, and he found he needed less and less insulin. As the weeks went by, his pain diminished, and before he reached the six-month mark, his pain was *gone*. This was something even medications could not promise, and yet simple changes in eating habits led to this amazing result.

▶ For Michael, a diet change saved his life. Over the years, his weight had gradually climbed to 330 pounds. After making the simple menu changes you'll read about here, he lost 160 pounds and is off all his medications. Needless to say, his doctor was thrilled. Now, Michael not only has his health back; he has his energy back. He enjoys long bike rides and feels good in his healthy new body.

Vance, Ashley, Selwyn, and Michael had something in common, aside from the fact that they faced health problems. They were all skeptical. At first, none of them was convinced that a menu change would really make much difference. After all, it wasn't as if they had really been eating all that badly. Could the nutritional tune-up I suggested really make much difference? And although they were certain that they wanted to give up weight problems, diabetes, and high blood pressure, they were not so sure about giving up favorite foods, and were certainly not prepared for a life of "deprivation."

As they soon found out, a dietary transition is life-changing in every sense of the word. They discovered new and exciting foods, and each one ended up in a new and much healthier body.

If these concerns resonate with you, hold that thought for a minute. *Everyone* is skeptical about the value of diet changes, and *everyone* worries about giving up favorites. So a focus in this book will be to make your menu change fit you like a sleek new glove.

What Are the Most Healthful Foods?

Scientific studies have shown that a healthful diet is based on these basic principles:

▶ The foods to emphasize each day are vegetables, fruits, whole grains, and legumes ("legumes" means beans, peas, and lentils).

▶ Meats, dairy products, eggs, and oily foods are unnecessary for health (and do considerably more harm than good) and should be excluded.

▶ Foods that cause a marked blood sugar rise—white bread, white potatoes, and sugar itself, for example— should be replaced by choices that are gentler on your blood sugar, such as rye or pumpernickel bread, yams and sweet potatoes, and fruits. These are known as low-glycemic-index (or low-GI) foods.

▶ It is important to include a source of vitamin B_{12}, such as any common multiple vitamin or fortified foods.

The recipes in this book are not only delicious and filling, they are low-fat, low-GI, and high in nutrients. You may be surprised by some of what we've tossed off the plate. Although some cookbooks include plenty of oils, sometimes singing the praises of extra-virgin olive oil, for example, we have found major advantages to using oil-free cooking techniques. Traces of oils are naturally found in vegetables, beans, fruits, whole grains, nuts, and seeds, of course. The problems start when these oils are bottled and sold in concentrated form and end up drenching our salads, pasta, and other dishes.

Oils are certainly better than animal fats. Beef fat, for example, is about 50 percent saturated fat—saturated fat is the "bad" fat that increases cholesterol levels and is linked to other health problems. About 30 percent of chicken fat is in the saturated form. Olive oil comes in at about 13 percent saturated fat. So cooking with olive oil is better than using chicken or beef fat, but is not nearly as good as sautéing your onions and garlic in water or vegetable broth so you can skip all that unnecessary "bad" fat.

If the absence of fish in these recipes comes as a surprise, it's good to remember that fish oil is a mixture, too. Yes, some of it is in the healthful omega-3 form, but most of the fat in fish is not omega-3 at all. It is a combination of saturated fat (usually between 15 and 30 percent) and a variety of other unnecessary fats that can expand your waistline and do your body no good.

Because fish are carnivores, small bits of mercury or other contaminants ingested by small fish become more and more concentrated as they are eaten by larger fish. And beyond unhealthful fats and contaminants, there is one more issue with fish: The protein in fish is not the healthful plant protein that is easy on your body. Animal protein—from cows, chicken, fish, or any other animal—tends to be hard for the kidneys to process, encouraging a gradual loss of kidney function. This is of most concern to people with diabetes, high blood pressure, or other conditions that may have already eroded their kidney health. But no matter who you are, a varied diet drawn from plant sources provides more than enough protein in its most healthful form.

So, skip the animal products and greasy, sugary foods, and enjoy the tastes and great health that vegetables, fruits, whole grains, and legumes can bring. As you page through the recipes in this book, you'll see that these powerful guidelines translate with remarkable ease into delicious foods.

Going for It: Take a Three-Week Test-Drive

If you do not yet follow a vegan diet, let me encourage you to incorporate more and more of these quick and delicious meals into your routine. And before too long, you should definitely give yourself a chance to try a vegan diet full-time and see what it can do for you. If that sounds like a big step, here's an easy way to give it a try:

First, leaf through these recipes and see which ones appeal to you. Make a few of them over the next week or two. The idea is not to change your overall diet yet; rather, you're just trying out some new foods. Check out the breakfasts, lunches, and dinners, so you are covering all your bases.

At the grocery store, you might also see what other foods meet these same nutritional guidelines (no animal products, minimal oil, low-GI), including convenience foods, such as cereals, canned soups, or frozen meals. Soon, you'll discover new favorites, including some that you will want to keep on hand for when you don't feel like cooking. Let yourself explore a bit.

Again, your goal is not to change your diet—not yet. Rather, you're just looking for the foods that fit our guidelines to see which ones you like best. I suggest you actually jot them down on a piece of paper with headings for breakfasts, lunches, dinners, and snacks.

What would you like for breakfast? How about Blueberry Pancakes (page 62) or a Marvelous Mango Smoothie (page 68)? How about soy yogurt? Maybe Sweet Potato Hash with Peppers (page 56)? You'll find all the recipes you need—and many more—in this book. Or maybe you'd prefer to just whip up some old-fashioned oatmeal, or zap some veggie sausage.

How about lunch? Want to start with Cajun Bean Soup (page 81) or Quinoa and Carrot Salad (page 82)? How about Wild Rice Pilaf with Roasted Garlic and Spinach (page 95) or Fire-Roasted Tomato Black Bean Chili (page 99)? Maybe Tempeh Sloppy Joes (page 84)? Or if you're out and about, fast-food places will be glad to serve you a bean burrito (hold the cheese), a veggie burger, or a veggie pizza (extra sauce, skip the cheese).

Dinner can be an elegant Fettuccine with Roasted Peppers and Zucchini (page 105) or a festive Three-Layer Tortilla Casserole (page 137)? Or maybe a simple dish, like Curried Tempeh Kabobs (page 116) or one of the many veggie pizzas (pages 117–123) in this book? If you're dining out, you'll find plenty of vegan choices at Italian, Chinese, Mexican, and Japanese restaurants.

For snacks, you'll want to keep fruit on hand, of course. But also try our dips, spreads, and the healthiest and tastiest popcorn you've ever tasted.

Write 'em down, try 'em out, and see which ones are keepers. Once you've found several recipes and products that you enjoy, you're ready for the next step: a three-week test-drive. Plan to have low-fat, healthful vegan foods for *every* meal, but for just three weeks. There's no major commitment, just a chance to see how things go.

For most people, these three weeks are an eye-opening experience. They start to lose unwanted pounds, their energy improves, and their digestion gets better. If they have diabetes, high cholesterol, or high blood pressure, these problems begin to improve, too. Headaches and joint pains start to melt away.

A three-week break from unhealthful habits sounds like a pretty small thing. But over and over, we hear from people whose lives are simply revolutionized:

"I never expected it would be this easy. I feel lighter, my skin glows, and I love the food."
JOYCE, MINNEAPOLIS, MN

"It took me a couple of days to get into it, but I have to say I wish I had done this 20 years ago. I am on half the medicines I was on two months ago, and now I'm working on the other half."
LINCOLN, CHICAGO, IL

"I have lost a total of 18 pounds. I run up and down my basement stairs with no pain in my knees at all."
SHERRI, ANCHORAGE, AK

"I have finally been able to lose the eight hanging-on pounds, while never being hungry."
NANCY, DENTON, TX

"I'm a five-year survivor of breast cancer. I wish I'd had this information when I was first diagnosed! I'm passing the info along to my daughters."
CORDE, PRINCETON, NJ

"This is the most important step I have ever taken. You have changed my life."
MANUEL, LOS ALTOS, CA

The other surprise is that your tastes change. Yes, it's true. Don't believe it? Well, let me draw on a common experience that illustrates what happens: Did you ever switch from whole milk to nonfat milk? At first, nonfat milk tastes watery. It doesn't even look right. But after a couple of weeks, what happens? You start to get used to the lighter flavor, and soon it tastes completely normal. And then, if you were to taste whole milk again, you would find it is much too thick—like cream.

Now, I am not suggesting that skim milk is health food. Rather, I use this common experience to show that our tastes change, often very quickly.

The same thing happens when you lighten your diet overall. At first, vegan foods may seem a bit light. But by the second week or so, you'll find that you enjoy their tastes and that they satisfy your appetite. And by the third week, if you were to have a double-bacon cheeseburger, you would find that it is not the culinary delight you had remembered. It is greasy and distasteful. In just a week or two, your body has moved in a healthful direction, and your taste buds have learned some new tricks.

"Can I have a little bit of cheese?" you might be thinking. "Maybe chicken every now and then?" Many people find themselves bargaining on behalf of their old favorite foods. But if you want the very best results, let me encourage you, for now, to not burden yourself with negotiating about how much or how little you will let unhealthful foods intrude into your new regimen. If you end up including a bit of cheese here and chicken there, you'll soon find that these foods elbow their way back into your routine, and you are right back where you started. Your body is changing and the way you view food is changing, too. So set aside foods that don't fit our healthy guidelines. You are better off not letting them tempt you.

Let these changes happen. As healthful foods become part of your routine, you will see what they can do for you.

Complete Nutrition

Just as your car needs the right fuel mixture to run well, your body needs the right nutrients, too. Protein, carbohydrate, fat, vitamins, and minerals—you need them all. So you may be wondering if you're getting everything you need.

Here's the bottom line: It turns out that the more low-fat vegan foods you add to your routine, the better your overall nutrition becomes. In our research studies, we carefully watch people's nutrition before and after major diet changes, and we find that a vegan menu brings tremendous improvements. Your plate frees itself of animal fat, cholesterol, and unnecessary calories, and serves up an abundance of vitamins and minerals.

While meat-centric diets are often low in fiber and several vitamins, and overdo it on fat and cholesterol, a vegan diet is just the opposite: It brings things into much better balance. Legumes and whole grains provide plenty of complete protein, without the cholesterol and fat found in meat, eggs, and most dairy products. And vegetables and fruits bring you vitamins, minerals, and natural plant compounds that a meaty diet just can't match.

Even so, three nutrients merit a bit of attention:

Calcium. For many people, calcium means dairy products. But dairy products bring you animal fat, animal protein, lactose sugar, cholesterol, and a sprinkling of hormones, none of which your body needs. More healthful sources of calcium are green leafy vegetables, such as broccoli, Brussels sprouts, kale, or collards, along with beans, peas, and lentils. Or, simply put, "greens and beans." Include these foods in your daily routine. One caveat, however: Spinach is different from most other greens in that its calcium tends to be poorly absorbed. In contrast, most other greens have highly absorbable calcium.

Iron. Green leafy vegetables and beans are also rich in iron. So that's another reason to include these great foods in your routine. Vitamin C increases iron absorption. So when citrus fruits, green peppers, or other vitamin-rich foods are consumed at the same meal as an iron-rich food, your body tends to take in more of the iron.

Vitamin B$_{12}$. Vitamin B$_{12}$ is essential for healthy nerves and healthy blood cells. You'll find it in some fortified foods, such as fortified soy milk, breakfast cereals, meat analogues, or nutritional yeast (look for the words "cobalamin" or "cyanocobalamin" on the labels), but the most convenient source is any standard multiple vitamin. It is essential to include a reliable source of vitamin B$_{12}$ in your routine.

Talk with Your Doctor

Be sure to talk with your health-care provider before making major changes to your diet or exercise routine. That is not because diet changes are risky. Quite the opposite; a change of the menu is often exactly what gets you back to health. But your provider can do any necessary diagnostic tests to check your health before you start and can track your progress along the way. If you are on medication for diabetes, high blood pressure, or cholesterol problems, sometimes diet changes can affect your medication needs. So your health-care provider can help you sort all these things out.

Join the Club!

As you discover what healthful foods can do, you'll want to take advantage of other resources. You'll find many listed in the back of this book, but there are a few I would like to emphasize.

At the Physicians Committee for Responsible Medicine, we have developed many programs to help people improve their eating habits. At our primary Web site, www.pcrm.org, you'll find books, answers to frequently asked questions, and even a weekly Webcast, called Food for Life TV. Our new 21-Day Vegan Kickstart Program will escort you into the healthiest possible diet with daily supportive email messages from doctors and celebrities. It's all free and waiting for you. You'll also have an opportunity to sign up for breaking medical news alerts and to join our organization and receive its quarterly magazine, *Good Medicine*.

At www.NutritionMD.org, health-care providers will find details on how foods affect everything from acne to varicose veins, and laypersons will find the same information in practical terms, along with a diet makeover program and nearly one thousand recipes, ready for you to explore.

At www.CancerProject.org, all the details on nutrition for cancer prevention and survival are presented in detail. You'll also find books and a directory to local vegan cooking classes.

At www.HealthySchoolLunches.org, you will find everything you need to help schools serve more healthful meals for children.

At www.NutritionCME.org, health professionals can earn continuing education credits for learning about good nutrition.

Good Luck!

We hope you enjoy these delicious tastes, and the new, healthy body that awaits you. Please share your new knowledge with others; you'll be a lifesaver. They will thank you, and so will we.

THE SCIENCE BEHIND A HEALTHFUL DIET

I (NEAL) GREW UP in Fargo, North Dakota, where the dietary staple was beef, and vegetables were not much more than an afterthought. The doctors in Fargo stayed busy treating heart disease, diabetes, high blood pressure, and other illnesses. Not that it is any different in any other North American town. Our not-so-healthful diets make it tough to stay slim and healthy.

In many parts of the world, however, things are very different. In Japan or China, for example, the traditional dietary staple is not beef. Rather, it is rice, along with plenty of vegetables. Meat is not a big part of their traditional diets. If used at all, it is added in small quantities, mainly as a flavoring for rice or noodles. Among some religious traditions, of course, meat is not consumed at all. As a result, people in these countries have been less likely to fall prey to obesity, cancer, or heart disease, compared with Americans. And, despite less availability of medical care, they live years longer than Americans do, as we saw in the introduction.

The difference is not due to genetics. When Asians change to a Westernized diet, as has been happening due to the influx of fast-food chains, they rapidly develop the same problems that have plagued Americans.

But how do we really know which foods are best? How can we tell for sure which ones help us slim down or live longer, and which ones can do us harm? What's the evidence?

Many researchers, including our own team at the Physicians Committee for Responsible Medicine, have tackled these questions over many years. In this chapter, I'll give you a glimpse in how this process works. In some cases, researchers have studied groups of people with different eating habits to see if one group is healthier than another. They might ask whether vegetarians tend to stay healthier than meat-eaters. Or do vegans do better than people who include dairy products and eggs on the menu? Then, when a certain food or dietary pattern shows promise, researchers test it out in specially controlled circumstances.

It Starts with Simple Observations

To tease out the effects of various ways of eating, researchers have been particularly keen on studying various groups of vegetarians and comparing them to meat-eaters. Among those who have been repeatedly put under the microscope are Seventh-Day Adventists. The reason is that Adventists are admonished to avoid tobacco, alcohol, caffeine, and meat. And while most Adventists observe the first three guidelines very well, only about half follow vegetarian diets; the other half include meat in their routines, albeit in rather modest amounts. The result is a natural experiment that has allowed researchers to see the effects of including or excluding meat in the diet in an otherwise health-conscious population.

In studies of tens of thousands of people, the vegetarians have clearly had the upper hand. They are slimmer than meat-eaters, have lower blood pressure, have much less risk of diabetes and other health problems, and they live longer.

In May 2009, researchers went a step further.[1] In a study of 60,903 Adventist adults, the research team was able to tease out the differences, not just between vegetarians and meat-eaters, but between five different diet groups: nonvegetarians, semivegetarians (having meat meals no more than once a week), pesco-vegetarians (fish-eaters), ovo-lacto-vegetarians (egg and dairy eaters), and vegans (who consume no animal products). In a report published by the American Diabetes Association in its journal *Diabetes Care*, the team reported that nonvegetarians were clearly the heaviest group. Semivegetarians and pesco-vegetarians were somewhat slimmer than typical meat-eaters, on average, but were nowhere near as slim as full-time vegetarians. And the only group that stayed well within the boundaries of a healthy weight was the vegan group. The researchers also found that diabetes risk followed exactly the same gradient. It was common in meat-eaters (7.6 percent of adults over age thirty), and fairly rare in vegans (2.9 percent).

Other studies showed much the same pattern. In the European Prospective Investigation into Cancer and Nutrition (EPIC), which included 37,875 participants, vegans were once again the trimmest, meat-eaters the fattest, and fish-eaters and ovo-lacto-vegetarians in between.[2] Virtually every study looking at body weight, cholesterol levels, or blood pressure has shown that people following plant-based diets have the advantage over their meat-eating friends.

Putting Foods to the Test

Observational research, such as the Adventist studies or the EPIC trial, is extremely valuable. But these studies cannot always establish cause and effect. Perhaps vegans might also tend to take better care of themselves overall, see their physicians more often, or have some other trait that might account for the difference.

So to put a vegetarian or vegan diet to a stricter test, researchers have asked people who were not yet following such a diet to make the switch, and have tracked their progress in carefully controlled studies. In some cases, they have studied specific combinations of healthy lifestyle changes, such as a combined diet and exercise program.

In what has become a classic study, Dr. Dean Ornish, a Harvard-trained physician, asked a group of heart patients to begin a low-fat vegetarian diet, along with other healthy lifestyle changes.[3] The results were astounding. Not only did their weight drop and their cholesterol levels fall dramatically; the artery blockages that had been worsening year after year, causing chest pain and, in some cases, threatening their lives, actually began to shrink. The tiny trickle of blood passing through the coronary arteries actually widened day by day, causing chest pain to dissolve almost like magic.

This had been thought to be impossible. Surgery was the only way artery blockages could ever shrink, doctors had assumed. But no, diet and lifestyle changes did this without the need for medicines or surgical procedures of any kind. Then a new report five years later showed that Dr. Ornish's patients never regained their lost weight, and they had cut their risk of any further heart problems in half.[4] If this had been a medicine, its patent would have been worth millions.

I learned about Dr. Ornish's research, and contacted him. I explained my concern that, while many doctors could be persuaded that his diet program was powerful, few would believe that most patients would be willing to try it. After all, the regimen meant giving up meat, most dairy products, fried foods, etc.— and some doctors presume that their patients would rather take medication than make substantial changes in their eating habits.

Dr. Ornish invited me to come to San Francisco to meet the research volunteers and interview them. We did this carefully, using a questionnaire that asked the volunteers how they felt about their diets, how much effort their new way of eating required, what they planned to do in the future, etc.[5] It turned out that the vegetarian diet did take a bit of getting used to—the research participants had had to learn a few new tastes and forget some old ones. But within a few weeks, they had gotten the hang of it. And because it had proved so effective—knocking out their chest pain, helping them lose weight, and giving them control of their health—they wanted to stick with it.

Dr. Ornish had a control group that was not asked to make diet changes. Rather, they were following whatever diets their personal physicians had recommended, which usually meant emphasizing chicken and fish, and we interviewed them as well. To our surprise, we found that they were not particularly happy with their diets. Many reported that chicken and fish were getting a bit old. Since their diet had brought virtually no benefit, they could not see what the point was.

The moral of the story seemed to be that people balk a bit at any new diet at first. But if the diet produces results, people embrace it heartily.

At the Cleveland Clinic, surgeon Caldwell Esselstyn, MD, took heart research a step further. He asked patients with severe heart disease to start a low-fat vegan diet. If the diet change did not reduce a patient's cholesterol level to below 150 mg/dL, he added a cholesterol-lowering medication. The diet-drug combination made his patients practically bulletproof. After twelve years, not a single individual who adhered to the regimen had any heart complications at all.[6]

Perhaps the results are not entirely surprising. After all, foods from plants do not have cholesterol or animal fat. Most animal products, on the other hand, have plenty of both, and they lack the soluble fiber that lowers cholesterol. For the participants, the results were life-changing.

In Toronto, Dr. David Jenkins took the research in a fascinating new direction, testing how quickly a plant-based diet slashes cholesterol levels.[7] His volunteers began a plant-based diet that emphasized specific foods with known cholesterol-lowering ability (the quantities listed are based on a 2,000-calorie diet):

1. Foods rich in soluble fiber, such as oats or barley: 20 grams
2. Soy protein from soy milk and soy meat analogues: 40 grams
3. Almonds: 28 grams
4. Special sterol- or stanol-enriched margarine (e.g., Benecol): 2 grams

A control group was prescribed a cholesterol-lowering medication instead of a diet change. After four weeks, the medication group cut its LDL ("bad") cholesterol by about 31 percent, which is a big drop. But in the same time frame, the diet group had accomplished nearly the same cholesterol-lowering—a 29 percent drop—without medications, using simple diet changes alone.

Meanwhile, a research team in Australia tested the effect of plant-based diets on blood pressure, finding that it lowers blood pressure within six weeks, both for people with high blood pressure and people who started with normal blood pressure.[8]

Cancer researchers began to use similar diets. Their question went beyond whether a healthy diet could prevent cancer. They wanted to know if diet changes could improve survival in people who had already been diagnosed with cancer.

The Women's Intervention Nutrition Study (WINS) included nearly 2,500 postmenopausal women who had previously been treated for breast cancer, asking them to reduce their intake of fatty foods.[9] Over the next five years, the risk of recurrence was cut by more than 20 percent. That was a start. A second study, called the Women's Healthy Eating and Living (WHEL) study tested the effects of boosting vegetables and fruits.[10] Over the next seven years, the women who ate at least five fruit and vegetable servings daily and who were also physically active had half the risk of dying, compared with those who either skipped their vegetables and fruits or missed regular exercise.

Putting these studies together, it may be that the best cancer-fighting regimen puts all of these healthy steps together: cutting the fat, boosting vegetables and fruits, and getting plenty of exercise.

Dr. Ornish did a study that tested something very much like this combination in ninety-three men with prostate cancer.[11] Using a low-fat, vegan diet, along with exercise and stress management, he found that the disease simply seemed to stop progressing for many of them, as judged by a blood test, called prostate-specific antigen, or PSA. In a control group that did not make diet changes, PSA levels gradually worsened, showing the usual progression of the disease. Other researchers have found similar benefits with plant-based diets in men with advanced prostate cancer.[12,13]

Why would healthy foods help people with cancer? The most likely reasons are that high-fiber, low-fat foods tend to reduce the blood levels of hormones that could otherwise promote cancer growth, along with beneficial effects of vegetables and fruits on anticancer defenses.

At our research center, we have tested plant-based diets for many conditions. We measured the weight-reducing effect of a low-fat vegan diet in a group of overweight women, all of whom were postmenopausal and had tried many diets before. We found that the menu change led to weight loss of about one pound per week, even without exercise or any limit on calories or portion sizes.[14] After two years of study, that lost weight never came back.[15]

A similar diet has a dramatic effect on diabetes, as I mentioned in the previous chapter. Our research volunteers found that their blood sugars improved, sometimes dramatically, their waistlines slimmed down, and their cholesterol levels fell.[16-20] Many needed less medication or were able to discontinue their medications altogether. And, compared to a typical diabetes diet that requires restricting portion sizes and counting carbohydrate grams, a low-fat vegan diet turns out to be pretty simple.

In a separate test, we also found that a low-fat vegan diet helps with menstrual problems, reducing menstrual pain and PMS.[21] Again, a beneficial effect on hormones is the likely explanation.

These advances have not gone unnoticed by scientific organizations. The American Diabetes Association published our findings in 2006, and has frequently invited me to present our findings at its annual scientific conferences. The American Dietetic Association has long held that low-fat vegan diets are nutritious and have many health benefits,[22] and has published several of our research reports in its journal.[23-26] In 2007, the American Medical Association called for more vegetarian foods in school lunches, a step that can help prevent many health problems.

Putting Healthful Foods to Work

Clinicians have been putting these healthful diet changes to work for their patients. In Santa Rosa, California, Dr. John McDougall has been using low-fat vegan diets for many years for individuals with heart problems, weight problems, diabetes, and many other conditions. His patients routinely lose weight, regain their health, reduce or eliminate medications, and begin living again.

Dr. Hans Diehl uses plant-based diets in the Coronary Health Improvement Project, an intensive four-week community-based program that provides in-depth instruction and support—and even works with local restaurants to feature heart-healthy foods. Participants report dramatic—often life-changing—results.

Of course, many people find out about the health benefits of plant-based diets on their own, without seeing a doctor or participating in a research study. Two of the most remarkable cases occurred, not in patients, but in athletes. Brendan Brazier is an ultramarathon runner and triathlete in top form. Early on in his career, he realized that all runners can push themselves to train hour after hour. What separated the winners from the also-rans was not their training regimens, but their recovery time between exercise bouts. By adopting a totally vegan diet, he found that he regained his energy more quickly than other athletes did and could resume training sooner.

Scott Jurek is one of the most amazing athletes ever born. In 1999, Scott won the Western States Endurance Run—a race that stretches, believe it or not, for a distance of 100 miles. He won the race again the next year. And the next, and the next—seven years in a row. His menu is a bit like that of a stallion or a gazelle, in the sense that he follows an entirely vegan diet, with no burgers or fried chicken to slow him down.

If you are aiming to win the marathon of life, you'll want to stick to healthy foods, too.

Despite the wealth of research on the benefits of vegan diets, some things are still not entirely clear. For example, is it a good idea to have most of your food raw, rather than cooked? If nuts are fatty—as indeed they are—is it better to avoid them or do their heart-health benefits trump any other considerations? Should you draw your staple foods mainly from grains and vegetables, with relatively little fruit, or is it better to go with lots of fruit? These are questions that, I hope, will be sorted out in the future.

While there is clearly much more to be learned, this book is based on the best available evidence, providing a wide variety of delicious meals that put the power of foods to work. Studies of people following vegetarian, especially vegan, diets have confirmed that we are much better off when animal products are off the menu.

People following plant-based diets are slimmer than their meat-eating friends. They are much more likely to remain healthy throughout life. And when people who have not followed an especially healthful diet finally move away from animal products and put a new emphasis on whole grains, vegetables, fruits, and legumes, their health often rebounds.

REFERENCES:

1. Tonstad S, et al. Type of vegetarian diet, body weight and prevalence of type 2 diabetes. *Diabetes Care* 2009;32:791–6.

2. Spencer EA, et al. Diet and body mass index in 38,000 EPIC-Oxford meat-eaters, fish-eaters, vegetarians, and vegans. *Int J Obesity* 2003;27:728–34.

3. Ornish D, Brown SE, Scherwitz LW, et al. Can lifestyle changes reverse coronary heart disease? The Lifestyle Heart Trial. *Lancet* 1990;336:129–33.

4. Ornish D, Scherwitz LW, Billings JH, et al. Intensive lifestyle changes for reversal of coronary heart disease. *JAMA* 1998;280:2001–7.

5. Barnard ND, Scherwitz LW, Ornish D. Adherence and acceptability of a lowfat vegetarian diet among patients with cardiac disease. *J Cardiopulmonary Rehabil* 1992;12:423–31.

6. Esselstyn CB, Jr. Updating a 12-year experience with arrest and reversal therapy for coronary heart disease (an overdue requiem for palliative cardiology). *Am J Cardiol* 1999;84:339–341, A338.

7. Jenkins DJ, Kendall CW, Marchie A, et al. Effects of a dietary portfolio of cholesterol-lowering foods vs lovastatin on serum lipids and C-reactive protein. *JAMA* 2003;290:502–510.

8. Rouse IL, Beilin LJ. Editorial review: vegetarian diet and blood pressure. *J Hypertension* 1984;2:231–40.

9. Chlebowski RT, Blackburn GL, Thomson CA, et al. Dietary fat reduction and breast cancer outcome: interim efficacy results from the Women's Intervention Nutrition Study. *J Natl Cancer Inst* 2006;98:1767–76.

10. Pierce JP, Stefanick ML, Flatt SW, et al. Greater survival after breast cancer in physically active women with high vegetable-fruit intake regardless of obesity. *J Clin Oncol* 2007;25:2345–51.

11. Ornish D, Weidner G, Fair WR, et al. Intensive lifestyle changes may affect the progression of prostate cancer. *J Urol* 2005;174:1065–70.

12. Carter JP, Saxe GP, Newbold V, Peres CE, Campeau RJ, Bernal-Green L. Hypothesis: Dietary management may improve survival from nutritionally linked cancers based on analysis of representative cases. *J Am Coll Nutr.* 1993;12:209–26.

13. Saxe GA, Hebert JR, Carmody JF, et al. Can diet in conjunction with stress reduction affect the rate of increase in prostate specific antigen after biochemical recurrence of prostate cancer? *J Urol* 2001;266:2202–7.

14. Barnard ND, Scialli AR, Turner-McGrievy G, Lanou AJ, Glass J. The effects of a low-fat, plant-based dietary intervention on body weight, metabolism, and insulin sensitivity. *Am J Med* 2005;118:991–7.

15. Turner-McGrievy GM, Barnard ND, Scialli AR. A two-year randomized weight loss trial comparing a vegan diet to a more moderate low-fat diet. *Obesity* 2007;15:2276–81.

16. Barnard ND, Cohen J, Jenkins DJ, Turner-McGrievy G, Gloede L, Jaster B, Seidl K, Green AA, Talpers S. A low-fat, vegan diet improves glycemic control and cardiovascular risk factors in a randomized clinical trial in individuals with type 2 diabetes. *Diabetes Care* 2006;29:1777–83.

17. Turner-McGrievy GM, Barnard ND, Cohen J, Jenkins DJA, Gloede L, Green AA. Changes in nutrient intake and dietary quality among participants with type 2 diabetes following a low-fat vegan diet or a conventional diabetes diet for 22 weeks. *J Am Diet Assoc* 2008;108:1636–45.

18. Barnard ND, Noble EP, Ritchie T, Cohen J, Jenkins DJA, Turner-McGrievy G, Gloede L, Ferdowsian H. D2 Dopamine receptor Taq1A polymorphism, body weight, and dietary intake in type 2 diabetes. *Nutrition* 2009;25:58–65.

19. Barnard ND, Gloede L, Cohen J, Jenkins DJA, Turner-McGrievy G, Green AA, Ferdowsian H. A low-fat vegan diet elicits greater macronutrient changes, but is comparable in adherence and acceptability, compared with a more conventional diabetes diet among individuals with type 2 diabetes. *J Am Diet Assoc* 2009;109:263–72.

20. Barnard ND, Cohen J, Jenkins DJ, Turner-McGrievy G, Gloede L, Green A, Ferdowsian H. A low-fat vegan diet and a conventional diabetes diet in the treatment of type 2 diabetes: a randomized, controlled, 74-week clinical trial. *Am J Clin Nutr* 2009;89(suppl):1588S–96S.

21. Barnard ND, Scialli AR, Hurlock D, Bertron P. Diet and sex-hormone binding globulin, dysmenorrhea, and premenstrual symptoms. *Obstet Gynecol* 2000;95:245–50.

22. American Dietetic Association. Position of the American Dietetic Association : vegetarian diets. *J Am Diet Assoc* 2009;109:1266–82.

23. Reilly JK, Lanou AJ, Barnard ND, Seidl K, Green AA. Acceptability of soymilk as a calcium-rich beverage in elementary school children. *J Am Dietetic Assoc* 2006;106:590–593.

24. Turner-McGrievy GM, Barnard ND, Cohen J, Jenkins DJA, Gloede L, Green AA. Changes in nutrient intake and dietary quality among participants with type 2 diabetes following a low-fat vegan diet or a conventional diabetes diet for 22 weeks. *J Am Diet Assoc* 2008;108:1636–45.

25. Barnard ND, Gloede L, Cohen J, Jenkins DJA, Turner-McGrievy G, Green AA, Ferdowsian H. A low-fat vegan diet elicits greater macronutrient changes, but is comparable in adherence and acceptability, compared with a more conventional diabetes diet among individuals with type 2 diabetes. *J Am Diet Assoc* 2009;109:263–72.

26. Barnett TD, Barnard ND, Radak TL. Development of symptomatic cardiovascular disease after self-reported adherence to the Atkins Diet. *J Am Diet Assoc* 2009;109:1263–5.

MAKING YOUR FOODS FIT YOUR GOALS

IF YOU ARE looking for recipes that will delight your taste buds and add wonderful variety to your menu, you've found them. We hope you'll want to try them all. But if you're thinking beyond taste and are targeting a specific health goal, you might go a step further, looking at which foods are the *best* choices for your condition, and why they work.

Let's say you want to knock off a few pounds. Or perhaps you want to bring down your blood pressure or cholesterol level. Maybe you're aiming to tackle diabetes. In the sections that follow, I'll describe how to adjust your menu for each of these goals, among others. While similar diet changes apply to all of these conditions, there are important differences in emphasis.

Slimming Down

"Losing weight is easy; the hard part is keeping it off." That's what people say, don't they? Well, I have a pleasant surprise for you. With the approach you are about to read, losing weight is easy, and keeping it off *is just as easy*. We are not talking about an old-fashioned calorie-counting diet that starves the weight off, only to see it boomerang back. Nor is it like a low-carbohydrate diet that wows you with quick initial weight loss, only to depress you with all-too-quick weight regain. No, our menu is designed to take the weight off and keep it off for good.

RENÉE

Renée was thirty-eight years old and had tried just about every diet you can think of. She had grown up in New Orleans and was not heavyset as a child. But during her freshman year in college, things began to change. She was as active as ever—even more so. She was on the women's basketball team. But she finished the year nearly 10 pounds heavier than she began it, which she attributed to the culture of pizza and fast food at her school. Over the next three years, she never shed those pounds. After graduation, she took a job as an on-air personality at a local television station. Her weight began to climb, for reasons she could not put her finger on. Eventually, she was 50 pounds heavier than she wanted to be. It affected her self-esteem, and she feared it might eventually affect her job, not to mention her health over the long run.

I met Renée during a book tour and introduced her to a program focusing on low-fat vegan foods. It was simpler than anything she had ever tried. No calorie counting. No portion sizes. No hunger. No carb limits. She did not think twice. She plunged in and gave it a try, e-mailing me every two weeks or so to let me know how things were going. Her weight dropped 2 pounds, 5 pounds, 8 pounds, 12 pounds, 15 pounds.

She often sent recipes that she and her husband had found and wanted to share, as well as surprising new restaurant offerings. This was not a diet; it was an adventure. It took about a year and a half for those 50 pounds to melt away, but she is now slightly thinner than she was when she started college, and her self-esteem and energy are back. Her husband lost close to 30 pounds, and is delighted, too.

Let me describe the foods we'll focus on, and then I'll explain why and how they work.

The two keys for weight loss are:

1. Steer clear of animal-derived products. This means eating plenty of whole grains, vegetables, fruits, and legumes (beans, peas, and lentils), and all the foods that are made from them, while avoiding meats, dairy products, and eggs.
2. Avoid added oils. Instead of sautéing in oil, you can sauté in water or vegetable broth. Instead of dribbling oily dressings all over your salad, go fat-free.

These two simple guidelines allow you to lose weight easily, without counting calories and without restricting carbohydrates at all.

Imagine, you'll savor stews, kabobs, crepes, and even cake, and still lose weight. Normally, we think of how tasty and satisfying these foods will be, rather than how nutritious they are. But they are just the kinds of foods that will trim down your waistline. Because weight control is such a common goal, we have designed every recipe in this book to fit these two guidelines. Enjoy them, and enjoy what they do for your body.

Can these simple steps really cause lasting weight loss? Absolutely yes. My research team put these menu changes to the test in several carefully controlled studies. One of these involved a group of sixty-four women. All of them were past menopause, all were overweight and had tried many different diets, and it is fair to say that they all felt stuck. We gave the women just two rules, the ones you read above—avoid animal products and oily foods. They were free to eat as much as they wanted of everything else (the recipes in this book would all have fit in perfectly). The study lasted fourteen weeks, and during that time the average participant lost about a pound per week. We then tracked everyone for the next two years. Unlike the usual dieter's experience, which is a rapid weight regain, we found that the average participant was still losing weight two years later!

HOW THESE RECIPES WORK
FOR WEIGHT LOSS

These seemingly magical foods have three properties that bring weight loss. They are modest in calories, they satisfy the appetite quickly, and they boost your metabolism after each meal. Here are the details:

Calories: Where are the calories in the foods you eat? Think about it for a second. A chicken stores calories in chicken fat. A cow stores calories in beef fat. A fish stores calories in fish oils. If any animal eats more food than is needed for energy, those extra calories do not end up as feathers or hooves. They are stored in body fat. So if you eat chicken fat, beef fat, or fish fat, you are eating the animal's calorie-storing tissues.

How many calories are we talking about? If you were to measure the calories in any of these kinds of fat—chicken fat, beef fat, or fish oil—you might be surprised to find that they are all exactly the same: Every gram of fat—no matter which animal it came from—holds 9 calories.

That is important to remember, because many people imagine that the fattening foods are carbohydrates—breads, rice, potatoes, etc. The fact is, a gram of carbohydrate has only 4 calories—less than half the calories in any kind of fat.

So, if you are aiming to lose weight, skipping animal products is a great first step. If you don't eat any chicken, beef, fish, or other meats, you will not get any of their stored calories. So the burgers in this book are totally vegan. There is not a scrap of an animal in the pizza recipes, either. Ditto for the delicious pasta dishes.

You might be thinking, well, what about *lean* meat? Is that okay? Sorry to depress you, but fat permeates animal muscle tissue, like water lurking in a damp sponge. Even if you trim away all the visible fat, there is still a sizable amount of fat lurking in that "lean" meat. You may not see it, but it is there.

Let's say you bought a chicken breast and threw away the skin and all visible fat. Still, as many as one-fourth of its calories come from fat hiding within the muscle tissue. So if your curry were made from chicken, instead of spicy vegetables, as it is in this book, you'd get a load of animal fat you never bargained for. Cholesterol lurks in the lean, too—there is actually more cholesterol in the lean portion of meats than in their fatty parts.

What about dairy products? Well, whole milk is about 49 percent fat, as a percentage of its calories. Typical cheeses are around 70 percent. These are both huge sources of fat and calories. And if you were to remove the fat—as in skim milk—the number one component is now *sugar*, believe it or not. Lactose sugar is the main source of calories in skim milk. That's why our delicious soups, salads, and even our raspberry cake are all dairy-free.

Vegetables, fruits, beans, and whole grains are a whole different story. Nearly all are very low in fat, which means that while they fill you up, they are naturally modest in calories.

One more thing: You'll notice that our recipes are not oily in the least. The reason is that vegetable oils have exactly the same number of calories as animal fats do. That's right: 9 calories in every gram, and that's true for the most expensive extra-virgin olive oil in the store and the cheapest bottle of corn oil. They all have 9 calories in every gram.

Now, there are tiny traces of natural oils in vegetables, fruits, beans, etc., and they are healthful. The trouble starts when oils are extracted—when olive oil is taken from olives, sunflower oil is removed from sunflower seeds, etc.—and are dribbled all over your pasta or salad, or cooked into French fries. The calories add up fast.

So avoiding animal products and added oils helps you steer clear of a lot of unneeded calories.

But, there are two other reasons why vegetables, fruits, whole grains, and beans are slimming:

Turning Off Your Hunger: Fiber—that is, plant roughage—fills you up before you have had very many calories. And although there is no roughage at all in animal products, there is plenty of it in plants. Think of high-fiber foods as a way to trick your brain into thinking you've eaten a lot of food, when, in fact, you have eaten quite sensibly.

Getting the "Burn": Finally, plant-based diets boost your calorie-burning machinery. Here is what this means: Normally, your calorie-burning speed increases slightly after a meal. As your body digests and processes the food you've taken in, some calories are given off as body heat, rather than being stored as fat. Scientists call this the thermic effect of food, or TEF. In our research, we have found that people who follow a vegan diet get an extra boost to their TEF. That is, their after-meal calorie burn is greater than before. The difference is modest, but real, and it gives you an extra edge.

So, the keys for losing weight are simple: steer clear of animal products and added oils, and choose from the delicious foods in this book. Without your being aware of it, you'll be avoiding excess calories, you'll feel full and satisfied, and your body will burn calories faster after meals. And you'll see the difference on the scale.

So many people have lost weight with this wonderful method. Many have tried every possible diet, and have been unable to keep the weight off. They are naturally skeptical that the *kind* of food they eat can make a difference. More likely, they have focused on the *amount* they eat, and if they find it tough to stick to a diet, they blame a lack of willpower. As you dig into these delicious recipes, it will all seem too good to be true. But within a matter of days, you will be convinced. Even as you dine on savory meals, the weight loss kicks in.

Many people are told by their doctors that weight loss would help their diabetes, bring down their cholesterol, or help in other ways. "Yes, but what about taste?" they ask. And here comes another surprise. As you slim down and improve your health, you discover tastes and aromas you never knew existed. You'll find yourself looking at meals in a whole different way. Your palate expands and you really *enjoy* eating again!

Healthy Heart, Lowering Cholesterol

MARTIN

Martin's father had a fatal heart attack at forty-two years of age. At age thirty-nine, Martin's cholesterol was 329 mg/dL—far above the 200 limit for a healthy cholesterol level set by the U.S. government.* His blood pressure was high, too: 150/103. And his doctor made it very clear that, if Martin continued to eat like his father, he was taking the same risks as his father. His doctor referred him to me. He had grown up in Wisconsin, and loved cheese, meat, and beer. As he sat in my office, I told him that, if he aimed to improve his health, he could keep one of those, and it was not going to be cheese or meat.

I had expected him to take this news rather hard. No more bratwurst. No more mozzarella sticks. And even beer had to be consumed intermittently and in modest amounts. But, in fact, he was thrilled. It gave him a way to escape what he had seen as a death sentence. I gave him the advice you will read here. He found it much more palatable than taking drugs for the rest of his life, and it turned out to be much more effective. Within a month, his cholesterol had fallen sharply, and his blood pressure was normal. Within three months, all his numbers were in the healthy range.

---

*Although the U.S. government advises that total cholesterol levels stay under 200 mg/dL, you will do well to aim at an even lower limit. A total cholesterol level of around 150 mg/dL is where heart attacks are nearly unknown. Low-density lipoprotein (LDL, or "bad") cholesterol should be below 100 mg/dL; some would say below 80 mg/dL. High-density lipoprotein (HDL, or "good") cholesterol should be above 45 mg/dL for men and above 55 mg/dL for women.

If your goal is to knock down your cholesterol, you can follow the same diet as for weight loss, avoiding animal products and steering clear of oily foods. Since your foods are free of animal fat and cholesterol, you're off to a great start. But why not go a step further? Certain foods have a specific cholesterol-lowering effect, and you can take advantage of it. The foods to emphasize are oats, fruits, beans, and certain vegetables, such as artichokes, broccoli, Brussels sprouts, carrots, green beans, sweet potatoes, winter squash. So our Spiced Pumpkin Oatmeal (page 65) and our Sweet Potato and Black Bean Brunch Burritos (page 66) will not just fill you up; they'll trim your cholesterol at the same time. Page through the recipes; you'll find many more with the same powerful ingredients.

HOW THESE RECIPES LOWER CHOLESTEROL

You may have seen advertisements claiming that oats—oatmeal or Cheerios, for example—can lower cholesterol. It's true, and here's how they do it: As your liver filters your blood, it removes some of the cholesterol and sends it into a tube, called the bile duct, which leads to your digestive tract. And there, oat fiber traps cholesterol and carries it out with the wastes.

However, there are actually many foods that have this effect. The secret is something called *soluble fiber*. It is what makes oats famous, and it is in a lot of other foods, too. It is in legumes—that is, beans, peas, and lentils. So every bite of our Lemony Lentil Vegetable Stew (page 87) or our Black Bean and Corn Salad with Lime (page 73) helps bring your cholesterol down a bit more. It is in barley, so our Berry Barley Soup (page 98) will trim your cholesterol, even as it delights your taste buds.

The cholesterol-lowering power of these foods is enormous. It is not at all unusual for a person with a cholesterol level that really worries his or her doctor to quickly bring it down to a level that makes his doctor proud, perhaps even envious.

Browse through the recipes; they are all free of cholesterol and animal fat. But you'll want to favor those with soluble fiber. The table opposite will tell you which ingredients to look for.

Top Foods for Soluble Fiber

FRUITS are rich in soluble fiber. You'll find it in apples, blackberries, figs, guavas, oranges, mangoes, peaches, pears, prunes, raisins, and many others.

OAT PRODUCTS (e.g., oatmeal and oat bran) are high in fiber. You'll also find it in some other grain products, such as raisin bran and barley.

BEANS and other legumes (chickpeas, navy beans, pinto beans, kidney beans, peas, soybeans, etc.) provide plenty of soluble fiber.

VEGETABLES are often high in soluble fiber. Good examples include artichokes, broccoli, Brussels sprouts, carrots, green beans, sweet potatoes, winter squash.

Sources: BW Li, KW Andrews, PR Pehrsson. Individual sugars, soluble, and insoluble dietary fiber contents of 70 high consumption foods, *J Food Composition and Analysis 2002;* 715:23, and Northwestern University, *NorthwesterNutrition* http://www.feinberg.northwestern.edu/nutrition/factsheets/fiber.html, accessed July 30, 2009.

If your concern is not cholesterol, but rather triglycerides, please take a look at the section on diabetes below, especially the part about low-glycemic-index foods. It turns out that these foods can trim triglycerides, too.

High Blood Pressure (Hypertension)

Going vegan and cutting the fat are also great for controlling blood pressure. People who have taken these steps usually see a nice drop in blood pressure. And if they have normal blood pressure to start with, these foods help it stay that way.

Part of the benefit of low-fat vegan foods comes from their effect on body weight. Slimmer people have lower blood pressure.

But these foods do more than that. They tend to make the blood less *viscous*—that is, less "thick"—less like grease and more like water. That means your heart does not need to push quite so hard to get your blood flowing through your arteries.

As you plan your menu, you'll want to pay special attention to vegetables and fruits. Meals that emphasize these healthful foods have an extra blood-pressure-lowering effect, as was proven in a major study called the Dietary Approaches to Stop Hypertension, or DASH, study. Some evidence suggests that vegetables' and fruits' blood-pressure-lowering ability is due to the fact that they are rich in potassium. So at mealtime, it's a great idea to put vegetables and fruits front and center.

Diabetes

If your goal is to tackle diabetes, everything you've read in this chapter so far applies to you. Foods with a slimming effect help bring diabetes under control, and an emerging body of research shows that avoiding fatty foods may also help your body regain some of its lost insulin sensitivity, as you may have seen in my book *Dr. Neal Barnard's Program for Reversing Diabetes*. Foods that cut cholesterol are essential, too. They minimize diabetes' assault on your heart.

But you have a couple more tricks up your sleeve. Certain foods give you extra power to control your blood sugar.

Low-GI foods. Let's say you had a serving of our Italian Fusilli with Sun-Dried Tomatoes and Artichoke Hearts (page 106). Enjoy it, savor it, and let it surprise you by having only a very modest effect on your blood sugar. The reason is the glycemic index.

The glycemic index is a number that shows which foods raise your blood sugar strongly, and which ones have much less effect. It was invented by David Jenkins, MD, PhD, a physician and researcher at the University of Toronto. White bread, for example, has a high glycemic index, which means that it tends to make your blood sugar rise significantly. Rye or pumpernickel, in contrast, have a low glycemic index. They have noticeably less effect on blood sugar.

Having said that, everyone is a bit different. If you find that a certain food tends to spike your blood sugar, you might set it aside for a while, and try it again later on.

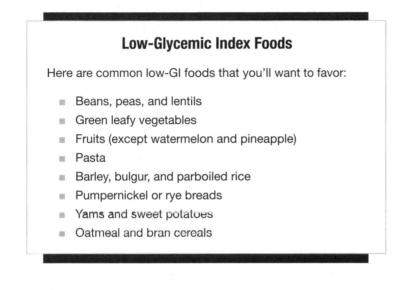

Low-Glycemic Index Foods

Here are common low-GI foods that you'll want to favor:

- Beans, peas, and lentils
- Green leafy vegetables
- Fruits (except watermelon and pineapple)
- Pasta
- Barley, bulgur, and parboiled rice
- Pumpernickel or rye breads
- Yams and sweet potatoes
- Oatmeal and bran cereals

Cinnamon. It turns out that cinnamon is good for healthy blood sugar, too. As little as ½ teaspoon of ordinary cinnamon each day can reduce blood sugar levels by 18 to 29 percent. So use it to top oatmeal or fruit desserts.

Cancer

For years, cancer researchers have been trying to understand why certain populations tend to stay free from cancer, while others have high cancer rates. Over and over, certain principles have emerged. First, people eating plant-based diets are less likely to develop cancer. Second, people already diagnosed with cancer who adopt plant-based diets tend to do better—that is, they are more likely to survive and less likely to need additional treatment. This has been shown for people with breast cancer and prostate cancer, and may also apply to colorectal cancer.

All the recipes in this book will be appropriate for those seeking cancer prevention or cancer survival. However, certain foods seem to have special value:

Vegetables and fruits. In the Women's Healthy Eating and Living Study, women who had been previously treated for breast cancer were more likely to survive over the long run if they ate plenty of vegetables and fruits *and* were physically active, as we saw in chapter 2. Also, the fiber in these foods helps prevent the formation of colon polyps—small growths that are the first step in colon cancer.

Soy. Soy products appear to help against breast cancer. Studies have shown that girls who consume roughly one serving of soy products (e.g., soy milk or tofu) each day are less likely to develop breast cancer in adulthood. Also, women previously diagnosed with breast cancer who consume soy products, such as soy milk, tofu, or edamame, tend to do better than women who avoid soy products. A 2009 report based on 5,042 women in the Shanghai Breast Cancer Survival Study showed that those who included soy products in their routine had a 32 percent lower risk of recurrence and a 29 percent decreased risk of death, compared with women who consumed little or no soy.

Soy is entirely optional, of course. But, if you would like to take advantage of its health power, allow us to suggest our Soy Yogurt Fruit and Granola Parfait (page 64), Edamame and Quinoa Salad (page 76), or Tempeh Burgers with Pineapple Salsa (page 83). You'll find several other soy recipes, too.

HOW THESE RECIPES HELP PREVENT CANCER OR IMPROVE SURVIVAL

Plant-based foods help fight cancer in several ways:

First, they are free of the cancer-promoting effects of meats and dairy products. Grilled chicken, for example, contains a chemical called PhIP, which arises as chicken (or any other muscle tissue) reaches grilling temperatures. The effect is specific to *muscle* tissue, so skip the grilled chicken and grilled salmon and have our Grilled Tofu with Smoky Barbecue Sauce (page 124) instead.

Likewise, dairy products increase the amount of IGF-I (insulin-like growth factor) in the bloodstream. IGF-I is linked to cancer, which may be why men who consume dairy products have high prostate cancer rates, compared with men who generally avoid dairy products. Our recipes are 100 percent dairy free.

Second, just as fiber-rich foods help the body eliminate cholesterol, as we saw above, they also help us eliminate excess hormones. And the mechanism is essentially the same: The liver removes hormones from the bloodstream and sends them into the digestive tract, where fiber carries them away. So while estrogens ("female sex hormones") can encourage the growth of breast cancer, fiber-rich foods help the body to eliminate hormone excesses. The same is true for the "male sex hormone"—testosterone—and prostate cancer.

Third, it may be that the antioxidants in fruits and vegetables (beta-carotene in carrots, lycopene in tomatoes and watermelon, and vitamin C in citrus fruits, for example) are able to protect our DNA from the kinds of damage that could lead to cancer.

Fourth, broccoli, Brussels sprouts, cauliflower, cabbage, and other *cruciferous* vegetables stimulate the liver to produce enzymes that neutralize chemical carcinogens that we are exposed to.

Fifth, soy products appear to have a particular anticancer benefit, although the biological explanation for it is not yet clear. Some have suggested that the very weak plant estrogens in soy attach to the estrogen receptors in a woman's body, blocking her natural (and much more powerful) estrogens from attaching and causing problems, but this is probably overly simplistic.

It is clear that plant-based diets help in a great many ways, and you will want to take full advantage their cancer-fighting power.

Digestive Problems

If your digestion is not what it should be, foods are usually the first place to look for problems, and for solutions.

If constipation is your problem, high-fiber foods can knock it out in no time. Meat, dairy products, and eggs have no fiber at all, which is why constipation is so common in meat-eating countries. But you'll find plenty of healthy fiber in plants. Beans are the fiber champions, followed by vegetables, fruits, and whole grains. Look through the recipe list, and you'll have no trouble picking out plenty of high-fiber choices. By the way, if beans cause gassiness, be sure to cook them until they are quite soft, and start with small servings.

Drugstores sell psyllium fiber (e.g., Metamucil) to relieve constipation. But it is actually made from the husks of seeds—essentially the same sort of fiber you would get if your diet contained vegetables, fruits, beans, and whole grains.

If you have the opposite problem—diarrhea and bloating, you may find that avoiding dairy products is a quick and easy solution. It works within about forty-eight hours. Lactose intolerance—the inability to digest the milk sugar lactose—is very common and totally normal. Soy milk, rice milk, and other non-dairy products will come to your rescue.

You may also want to favor rice. Rice dishes are very well tolerated, even by sensitive stomachs. If you have irritable bowel syndrome or inflammatory bowel disease, it is likely to be easier to digest than wheat, rye, or oats. So you might try our Ginger Tofu (page 145), our Caramelized Onions with Lentils and Brown Rice (page 114), our Stuffed Portobello Mushrooms with Brown Rice and Tomatoes (page 132), or our delicious Brown Rice, Chickpea, and Vegetable Soup (page 138).

Whatever your goals, all the recipes in this book are a great starting point. And with the guidelines in this chapter, you can zero in on the recipes that give you the strongest health benefits.

ALL ABOUT OUR RECIPES AND INGREDIENTS

COOKING WITHOUT ANIMAL products isn't really that much different from the cooking you may be used to. Well, maybe just a little different. But certainly it's not hard and with a little imagination, you will turn your kitchen into a vegan cooking haven! You will not miss out on flavor, either. Grains, beans, fruits, and vegetables lend themselves beautifully to seasonings like herbs, spices, flavored vinegars, exotic condiments, and more.

In fact, vegan cooking can be actually easier than cooking a meat-centered diet. There is no need for guessing whether the meat is cooked thoroughly enough. And cleanup is quick; no more after-meal battles with grease-encrusted pans. And you'll be glad to be rid of the risks of having raw meat on your countertop and cutting board. Cooking with beans, grains, fruits, and vegetables just means putting in a little care and love to have fantastic meals that are a snap to prepare.

It's Easy

We've purposefully designed recipes that can be prepared fairly quickly—in thirty minutes or less—and some are really speedy.

And for anything that might take longer, if you look carefully, most of that time is hands-off time, so you have time to even get in a fast run on the treadmill!

Most of our ingredients are easily found in any market—fresh produce, pasta, beans, rice, and simple flavorings and spices. Occasionally, we will introduce you to foods that may be new to Western palates—tempeh or tofu, for example. They add interesting flavors and plenty of good nutrition. And we will give you a listing of our favorite vegan products when cooking is simply out of the question—see page 211.

In our recipes, first and foremost we believe in quality. As you shop, take a few minutes to inspect your produce carefully. Look for the best pieces of fruit and vegetables. Go to the farmers' markets for a better selection if you need to. Stock up on beans and grains and keep them fresh in airtight containers. And, although we know you are busy, carve out some time to prepare a dish or two in advance of a hectic week so you are always prepared.

Stocking Your Kitchen: The Essentials

Preparing a healthful pantry is not hard and you might even already have the beginnings of a great one.

Many items you might cook with now are perfectly fine—canned chopped tomatoes, broth, grains, beans, pastas, soy sauce, and other condiments.

Here are some of the key foods to keep on hand so you'll always be able to whip up a quick recipe—and so those recipes will turn out fantastic!

SEASONINGS AND CONDIMENTS

Salt and pepper. Most of our recipes call for some salt and pepper. You may omit them, if you prefer. If you do use salt, we recommend **kosher salt** for most of your cooking, since you only need a dash to make the natural flavors of the foods come alive. **Sea salt** is also recommended, in particular for cold foods. The intense flavor is magic for foods that require no heat. As for pepper, throw out those jars of preground pepper and use a peppermill. **Freshly ground pepper** is really the only way to go.

Herbs and spices. When we call for an herb or spice, we'll let you know when it should be fresh. When using dried spices and herbs, take the sniff test. There should be a pretty powerful scent emanating from the bottle. Spices that are more than one and a half to two years old really should get the heave-ho.

You will notice we like spices that are typical in international cooking, such as **curry powder** or **cumin**. If you have been just a salt and pepper person for a long time, don't be afraid to try some new spices. Bold, powerful spices really jack up the flavor of beans and grains. The beauty of vegan cooking is that many of the featured ingredients act as canvasses for interesting spices and herbs, so dive right in and try them.

One of our favorite sources (besides the good old supermarket) for great dried spices and herbs is Penzey's (www.Penzeys.com). Their spices are some of the finest you will ever use.

Zest of citrus fruits. The skin, or zest, of lemons and oranges adds a wonderful rich, deep flavor to many foods. If you've never zested a peel before, it's easy with the right equipment. We suggest you purchase a Microplane grater, a long, sticklike, handheld grater with fine holes that is perfect for zesting. It's far superior to the box grater for this task. Microplanes can be found at most supermarkets, kitchen shops, cookware sections of home stores, and online.

Soy sauce. Soy sauce remains one of America's favorite condiments. Low-sodium varieties are available. There are lots of companies to choose from but we particularly enjoy the San-J brand, available in just about any supermarket. Tamari is a variant of soy sauce that is typically free of grains (typical soy sauce is made from soy and wheat), and contains no caramel coloring or artificial flavors. It has a nice, smooth, clean taste.

Hoisin sauce. Think of the way Americans use ketchup and you will find your Chinese equivalent in hoisin. While hoisin does contain sodium, it's so rich and flavorful, just a dab will do. Hoisin is made from beans, and its thick paste adds a smoky taste to foods. And for those of you who miss the barbecued flavor of grilled meat, hoisin can step in and make vegan cuisine just as delicious.

BEANS, GRAINS, AND PASTAS

Aaaaah . . . the backbone of healthy cuisine! Incorporating beans, grains, and some pastas in your food plan will give you endless delicious options.

Beans. Okay, we're bean happy! You will find a bevy of bean recipes in this book. Beans are among the most inexpensive and most nutritious ingredients. They are loaded with fiber, calcium, and iron.

Does cooking beans from scratch sound time-consuming? Well, they pretty much cook themselves! You just soak them overnight, change the water, and boil them until very soft, generally 1 to 3 hours, depending on the variety. You may also wish to keep some canned beans on hand, as they are convenient and ready anytime the mood strikes you. Just be sure to rinse them—rinsing canned beans reduces sodium by about one-third—or purchase no-salt-added canned beans.

If you have trouble digesting beans, start with small servings—a little bit goes a long way. And be sure they are very well cooked. You may also wish to cook dry beans with kombu, a sheetlike, green sea vegetable that is sold dried at natural food stores. Add about a 2-inch piece to cooking water. It helps in the digestion of the beans.

Grains. Whole grains are nutritious and satisfying; they give you protein, healthy carbohydrate, and plenty of fiber, not to mention delicious and varied tastes.

This book highlights brown rice, quinoa, wheat berries, whole wheat couscous, and polenta. As you'll see, we have kept things simple so as not to overwhelm you, choosing grains that are easy to find in a regular supermarket and that the whole family—including kids—will enjoy.

For all products except couscous, rinse grains in a fine sieve under cold running water for about one minute. This releases the excess starch so that cooked grains will remain more separated.

Brown Rice. Short-grain brown rice cooks to a stickier texture, and so it is good for times you want chewier rice. Use long-grain brown rice when you want a fluffier rice. One of our favorite brands of rice is Lundberg, a California producer of quality rice products, including organic varieties.

RICE COOKERS

To our minds, the rice cooker is one of the world's greatest inventions! For those of you who have ever burned rice on the stove or had it come out watery or mushy, how about a machine that cooks perfect rice every time? You can also use rice cookers for other whole grains, such as barley, quinoa, or wheat berries, and for steaming vegetables. You will find inexpensive rice cookers at Asian supermarkets and at cookware stores.

Quinoa. Quinoa (pronounced KEEN-wah) is one of our favorite grains. Discovered by the Incas some five thousand years ago, it's high in protein and fiber and cooks up in just 15 minutes! The texture is light and fluffy, but a nice, slightly crunchy texture. You'll find it used in cold and hot dishes in this book. It's so versatile.

Couscous. Couscous is a Moroccan pasta. We recommend whole wheat versions, which supply more fiber. They take no more time to cook than regular varieties, and offer a nutty flavor and hearty texture.

Pastas. Take a look at the new varieties of whole-grain pastas and Asian noodles. The days of grainy, heavy pasta are gone. One of our favorites is Healthy Harvest from Ronzoni. It has a tad of unbleached flour along with the goodness of whole wheat, so it will give you more fiber than regular pasta, but it is still light and delicious.

You will also want to try udon and soba noodles. Udon noodles are made from brown rice and are lighter in texture than soba noodles. Soba noodles are traditionally made from buckwheat and have a heartier flavor that goes especially well in soups. You can find them in the Asian aisle of many regular supermarkets.

CANNED AND BOTTLED GOODS

Canned tomatoes. We love fresh tomatoes. But with the exception of a few places in the United States where tomatoes are pretty good year-round, you wouldn't want to go near a tomato in January! So canned tomatoes are perfectly acceptable and make many dishes come alive with their earthy flavors. Our favorite brand is Muir Glen Organic Tomatoes. Their Fire Roasted Tomatoes taste like they have just come off the grill!

Vegetable broth. Some of our recipes call for vegetable broth (there is no need for chicken or beef broth), which we often use in place of oil for sautéing. It's nice to always have convenient canned or boxed vegetable broth on hand—we like the Swanson, Health Valley, and Pacific Foods of Oregon brands. But try making your own sometime. Here is an easy recipe that freezes well, so you can always have vegetable broth when you need it.

YOU MADE IT YOURSELF VEGETABLE BROTH

■ MAKES ABOUT 2 QUARTS

2 large yellow onions, coarsely chopped, skins included

2 large carrots, peeled and coarsely chopped

2 leeks, washed and coarsely chopped

1 parsnip, peeled and coarsely chopped

1 slice lemon

Handful parsley sprigs

Salt to taste

Combine all ingredients with 9 cups of water in a large stockpot and slowly bring to a simmer over low-medium heat. Partially cover and simmer for 2 hours. Strain the broth through a mesh strainer and press down on the vegetables to get all the liquid out. Freeze in ice cube trays or a 1-quart container for up to 3 months or store in the refrigerator in a covered container for up to 4 days.

Vinegars. Vinegars have always lent great flavor to food without extra calories, fat, or sodium. Try a variety of vinegars, such as champagne, herb, red, white, sherry, and raspberry. They stay fresh for up to a year.

You are probably familiar with most of the vinegars we use in these recipes, but there is one relatively new product you will enjoy: **balsamic syrup** or glaze is balsamic vinegar that has been boiled down to produce a rich, almost maple syrup–like texture. In the process, the "sting" of the vinegar is replaced with a smooth, sweet flavor that stands on its own beautifully. We like to drizzle it onto cooked foods. And when it comes to salad, you can get by with just this delicious glaze (no need for oil).

Roland (www.rolandfoods.com) makes a balsamic glaze, or you can easily make your own. Boil good-quality balsamic vinegar (look for brands that have aged at least five years) in a saucepan until reduced by half. Then add a teaspoon of sugar for each ½ cup of the original amount of vinegar, and boil down until the vinegar is thick, like syrup. Store in an airtight container.

Mirin. Also known as rice wine, mirin is thicker and smoother than rice vinegar. Although some people use mirin and rice vinegar interchangeably, mirin has a less tart flavor. It is easy to find; many major supermarkets have it on their shelves.

Agave nectar. This is our sweetener of choice. On the market now for several years, agave nectar is like a cross between honey and maple syrup in both its taste and texture. Agave nectar does not raise your blood sugar as dramatically as refined sugars, and it works very well in both cold and hot food preparation. It comes in light and dark varieties; we will specify which one to use for what purpose. Agave nectar is widely available nowadays; you will have no trouble finding it.

We are not fans of low-calorie sweeteners (e.g., Splenda, NutraSweet, etc.), but you might want to try stevia, a natural sweetener used in Europe for years and now available in the United States. It is marketed under the brand name Truvia and can be found at many major supermarkets.

OTHER PANTRY STAPLES

Dried mushrooms. Now here's a product that will stay fresh well beyond most of your pantry items. While we adore fresh mushrooms, dried mushrooms are so handy to have on hand and can be less expensive as well. Fresh porcini mushrooms, for example, are hard to come by in the United States, and they are mushrooms worth including in many dishes. They are rich in flavor, with a meaty texture and taste. Also look for dried shiitakes (also known as black mushrooms), morels, wood ear mushrooms, and other varieties. Keep a few on your shelves to slip into soups for an extra flavor boost.

Panko bread crumbs. For some of our recipes using bread crumbs, we've kicked the dusty, almost-too-ground-up, canned, traditional bread crumbs in favor of the rough-cut Japanese bread crumbs. These bread crumbs absorb flavors so much better, look better, and have a wonderful crunchy texture. Look for whole wheat panko.

Nutritional yeast. Say cheese! Okay, it's not really cheese, but nutritional yeast can be sprinkled on sauces, casseroles, popcorn, and just about anything where a cheeselike flavor would be welcome. Not to be confused with baker's or brewer's yeast, nutritional yeast is a mustard-colored yeast. It is high in protein and fat free, and some brands are enriched with vitamin B_{12}. Look in the supplement aisle of your nearest health-food store.

REFRIGERATED NONDAIRY PRODUCTS

Nondairy milks. Soy, rice, and almond milks do well in recipes that would otherwise call for cow's milk. Soy milk is the strongest flavored, followed by almond milk. Rice milk is quite mild. Experiment with these or others (e.g., oat milk, hemp milk, etc.) in your cooking to see what you like best. Or have a family taste test. Favorite brands include Silk soy milk, Rice Dream rice milk, and Blue Diamond Almond Breeze.

Vegan cheeses are still a work in progress, but you might like to try vegan soy Parmesan or vegan cream cheese while you transition to lighter tastes. Look for them in the refrigerated section of your supermarket.

"FAST FOOD"

For fast food anytime, we suggest keeping these staples on hand:

▶ hummus for wraps and sandwiches
▶ low-fat refried beans to spread on tortillas

▶ salsa to mix with black beans and frozen corn for a speedy chili

▶ soy milk or rice milk with muesli or bran cereal

The idea is to have on hand what you need. A well-stocked pantry makes healthful cooking *so* easy.

RECIPES

AND *MENUS*

PART 2

5

BREAKFAST

LET'S HAVE BREAKFAST! If you're looking for something quick and easy, you'll find it here. Try a Creamy Fruit Smoothie (page 164) or Spiced Pumpkin Oatmeal (page 65). And if you'd like a leisurely weekend breakfast, you'll have no shortage of choices, all of them as healthful as they are delicious.

Breakfast gives you a chance to start off your day on the right foot. For many people, unfortunately, eggs, bacon, and sausage carry a load of saturated fat and cholesterol onto their plates. And some people race off to work with no breakfast at all, leaving them low on energy all morning. Even worse, hunger may drive them to indulge in not-so-healthy snacks well before lunchtime. Studies show that people who skip breakfast actually end up eating *more* over the course of a day and have higher cholesterol levels, compared to people who start their day with breakfast.

It is *so* easy to have a healthy, delicious breakfast. It takes no more time, and your body will thank you many times over.

So enjoy our Spiced Pumpkin Oatmeal. It is hearty and delicious, and it naturally lowers cholesterol. *All* our breakfasts—just like everything in this book—are free of animal products. So even indulgent-sounding Vanilla French Toast (page 61), Banana-Ginger Pancakes (page 57), and Sweet Potato and Black Bean Brunch Burritos (page 66) are as healthful as they are delicious.

These breakfasts will satisfy your hunger, allowing you to resist unhealthful temptations you may encounter later in the day, and give you the energy you need to think, work, and feel great.

low carb

GREEN CHILE AND OYSTER MUSHROOM CREPES

MAKES 8 SERVINGS ■ **PREPARATION TIME: 5 minutes** ■ **COOK TIME: 45 minutes**

You will be delighted with this delicious savory spin on crepes. Mixing the batter is a cinch, and a nonstick pan practically guarantees success with this recipe.

1 tablespoon Ener-G Egg Replacer

½ cup plus 2 tablespoons soy creamer

¼ teaspoon salt

1 cup unbleached all-purpose white flour

Vegetable oil cooking spray

2 cups chopped oyster mushrooms

1 tablespoon chopped fresh sage plus extra for garnish

Black pepper to taste

2 to 4 tablespoons canned roasted diced green chiles

1. Mix the Ener-G Egg Replacer with ¾ cup water. Combine this with the soy creamer and salt. Quickly whisk the flour into the wet ingredients until completely smooth. The batter should be thin. If it is not thin, add another 1 to 2 tablespoons water.

2. Heat a nonstick pan over medium heat. Coat lightly with the vegetable cooking spray. Pour ¼ cup of the batter into the pan and quickly tilt and rotate the pan until the crepe batter is spread thin. Cook the first side for about 2 minutes until lightly browned at the edges and then loosen the crepe with a spatula. Flip it and cook the other side for about 1 minute. Set finished crepe aside and repeat with the remaining batter. Keep the crepes warm while working on the filling.

3. Sear the mushrooms over high heat in 2 tablespoons of water for 2 to 3 minutes. Add 1 tablespoon of the sage and black pepper to taste. Cook for 1 more minute until mushrooms are cooked through. Add the green chiles to the mushroom mixture and mix to combine.

4. Load about 2 tablespoons of the filling toward one side of the crepe, spreading it along the length. Roll the crepe closed and repeat until they are all filled, garnishing with sage.

DID YOU KNOW?

The batter for these crepes works well with sweet or savory dishes. Try a sweet filling, like strawberries or blueberries.

PER SERVING (⅛ OF RECIPE):		
86 calories	2.2 g protein	89 mg sodium
1.5 g fat	15.7 g carbohydrate	11 mg calcium
0.1 g saturated fat	1.7 g sugar	1.1 mg iron
15.8% calories from fat	0.9 g fiber	1.3 mg vitamin C
0 mg cholesterol		7 mcg beta-carotene
		0.2 mg vitamin E

POTATO HASH with PEPPERS

This recipe is a healthy spin on an old breakfast favorite. By using sweet potatoes, you'll be packing in a little extra flavor. The sweet paprika really enhances this dish for a sweet, savory meal.

2 pounds sweet potatoes, peeled and cut into ½-inch pieces

¼ cup vegetable broth

3 garlic cloves, minced

1 small onion, chopped

1 small red bell pepper, chopped

1 small green bell pepper, chopped

1 tablespoon sweet paprika

Kosher or sea salt to taste

Freshly ground black pepper to taste

1. Place sweet potatoes with water to cover in a large saucepan. Simmer potatoes for about 15 to 17 minutes until just tender. Drain and set aside.

2. Heat broth in a large skillet over medium heat. Cook garlic, onion, and bell peppers for about 4 minutes. Add paprika, salt, and black pepper and continue to cook for 5 minutes, until vegetables are soft. If necessary, add 1 to 2 more tablespoons broth. Add the sweet potatoes and cook to heat through.

DID YOU KNOW?

Cutting sweet potatoes into smaller pieces actually decreases cooking time and allows for more flavor to be absorbed.

PER SERVING (⅙ OF RECIPE):

107 calories	2.3 g protein	220 mg sodium
0.4 g fat	24.8 g carbohydrate	42 mg calcium
0.1 g saturated fat	8.7 g sugar	1.3 mg iron
3.1% calories from fat	3.9 g fiber	46 mg vitamin C
0 mg cholesterol		11678 mcg beta-carotene
		1.7 mg vitamin E

BANANA-GINGER PANCAKES

MAKES FOUR 3-PANCAKE SERVINGS ■ PREPARATION TIME: 10 minutes ■ COOK TIME: 20 minutes (depends on skillet size)

These delightfully spiced pancakes are a hearty fruit-flavored treat for breakfast or brunch.

1¼ cups whole wheat pastry flour

2 teaspoons baking powder

1½ teaspoons ground ginger

¼ teaspoon salt

2 tablespoons agave nectar

1¼ cups vanilla soy milk

3 tablespoons unsweetened applesauce

1 teaspoon vanilla extract

1 cup mashed bananas

Vegetable oil cooking spray

1. In a medium bowl, combine the flour, baking powder, ginger, and salt. In another bowl, combine the agave nectar, soy milk, applesauce, and vanilla. Add the liquid to the flour mixture. Mix until just combined (the batter will be lumpy). Add the bananas.

2. Heat a large skillet over medium heat, then coat with cooking spray. Pour ¼ cup of batter onto the hot skillet. The pancake is ready to flip when tiny bubbles appear on the top and burst, and the pancake is lightly browned on the edges. Flip the pancake and cook for about 1 to 2 minutes, until the underside is lightly browned. Adjust your heat so that the pancakes cook for about 1 to 2 minutes per side.

DID YOU KNOW?

One of the most popular condiments in the Philippines is banana ketchup, a sauce made of mashed bananas, vinegar, salt, and spices.

PER SERVING (3 PANCAKES):

268 calories	8.6 g protein	442 mg sodium
2.2 g fat	57.4 g carbohydrate	267 mg calcium
0.4 g saturated fat	16.7 g sugar	3.2 mg iron
6.9% calories from fat	7.1 g fiber	5.3 mg vitamin C
0 mg cholesterol		19 mcg beta-carotene
		1.6 mg vitamin E

SPICY SPINACH FRITTATA

low carb

MAKES 8 SERVINGS ■ **PREPARATION TIME: 10 minutes** ■ **COOK TIME: 20 minutes**

Frittatas are great for breakfast or brunch. This recipe is hearty, filling, and can easily be doubled for family or friends.

1 pound raw spinach

¼ cup soy creamer

⅓ cup vegetable broth

2 medium potatoes, chopped into ½-inch cubes

2 garlic cloves, minced

16 ounces extra-firm tofu, crumbled

⅛ teaspoon turmeric

⅛ teaspoon salt

¼ teaspoon freshly ground black pepper

⅛ teaspoon chipotle chili powder

1. Remove the spinach leaves from stems. Reduce spinach until it is thoroughly wilted by sautéing in a large pan on medium heat with the soy creamer and vegetable broth. Once the spinach is reduced, add the potatoes and garlic. Cook until potatoes are soft, about 15 minutes.

2. Preheat the oven to 375°F while the potatoes and garlic are cooking.

3. Purée half the tofu with turmeric, salt, black pepper, and chipotle powder in a food processor. Crumble the other half. Combine puréed tofu, remaining crumbled tofu, and spinach mixture in a 6 x 6-inch baking dish and mix thoroughly. Bake for 20 minutes. Remove the frittata from the oven and allow it to set for at least 10 minutes before serving.

DID YOU KNOW?

Using a cast-iron skillet can cut down on cleaning extra pots and pans because you can sauté and bake in your skillet. This frittata can go right from the stovetop to the oven.

PER SERVING (⅛ OF FRITTATA):

108 calories	7.6 g protein	110 mg sodium
4 g fat	12.6 g carbohydrate	160 mg calcium
0.4 g saturated fat	1.7 g sugar	3.2 mg iron
31.2% calories from fat	2.3 g fiber	10 mg vitamin C
0 mg cholesterol		2198 mcg beta-carotene
		0.8 mg vitamin E

SPANISH-STYLE SCRAMBLER WRAP

MAKES 4 WRAPS ■ **PREPARATION TIME: 5 minutes** ■ **COOK TIME: 10 to 12 minutes**

This delicious and filling faux-egg wrap is good enough to serve to the most traditional breakfast seekers. Serve with a side of black beans and plantains for an authentic Latino feel.

1 green bell pepper, seeded and chopped

1 small onion, chopped

12 ounces extra-firm tofu, crumbled

½ cup low-sodium vegetable broth

1 teaspoon chili powder

1 teaspoon ground cumin

1 teaspoon turmeric

1 pound fresh spinach

½ cup salsa

4 (8-inch) whole wheat tortillas

1. Heat ½ cup water in a nonstick skillet. Add the bell pepper and onion and sauté until the onion is translucent.
2. Add the tofu, ¼ cup broth, chili powder, cumin, and turmeric. Sauté, stirring often, for 5 to 7 minutes, or until done to your liking. Add spinach and remaining ¼ cup broth and cook 1 minute.
3. Add salsa and stir.
4. Divide the tofu mixture evenly among the tortillas and wrap it up.

DID YOU KNOW?

Pressing tofu really helps get a nice, chewy consistency. Here's how to do it: drain the tofu and place it between two plates with a heavy bowl or book on top. Let it sit for 30 minutes to an hour, drain the plate, and you are done.

PER WRAP:

213 calories	15 g protein	484 mg sodium
6.8 g fat	28.8 g carbohydrate	276 mg calcium
0.8 g saturated fat	4 g sugar	6 mg iron
26.7% calories from fat	6.4 g fiber	30.4 mg vitamin C
0 mg cholesterol		4625 mcg beta-carotene
		2.4 mg vitamin E

didn't eat ww tort

ALL-AMERICAN SCRAMBLE ON PUMPERNICKEL BAGEL

MAKES 4 SERVINGS ■ **PREPARATION TIME: 15 minutes** ■ **COOK TIME: 10 minutes**

Who doesn't enjoy a leisurely Sunday morning breakfast? Here's one for the whole family, a delicious tofu scramble with all the fixings on a toasted pumpernickel bagel.

1 green bell pepper, seeded and chopped

1 small onion, chopped

½ cup sliced mushrooms

12 ounces extra-firm tofu, drained and pressed

1 tablespoon nutritional yeast

1 teaspoon turmeric

½ teaspoon freshly ground black pepper

4 pumpernickel bagels

4 slices vegan cheese (optional)

1. Heat ½ cup water in nonstick sauté pan. Add the bell pepper, onion, and mushrooms and sauté until the onion is translucent. Add the tofu and sauté, stirring often, for 5 to 7 minutes, or until done to your liking. Add the nutritional yeast, turmeric, and black pepper and stir.

2. Toast the bagels, divide the scramble evenly among the bagels, and top with a vegan cheese slice, if using.

DID YOU KNOW?

Pumpernickel bread has a lower glycemic index than typical wheat breads, which means it's gentler on your blood sugar.

PER SERVING (¼ OF RECIPE):

418 calories	18.5 g protein	361 mg sodium
6.2 g fat	74.6 g carbohydrate	175 mg calcium
0.6 g saturated fat	10.4 g sugar	5.5 mg iron
12.5% calories from fat	7 g fiber	22.9 mg vitamin C
0 mg cholesterol		76 mcg beta-carotene
		0.4 mg vitamin E

VANILLA FRENCH TOAST

MAKES SIX 2-SLICE SERVINGS ■ **PREPARATION TIME: 10 minutes** ■ **COOK TIME: 20 minutes**

Start your weekend off right with this delicious French toast that is simple to prepare and oh-so-tasty. Serve with sliced fresh fruit.

8 ounces low-fat silken tofu

½ cup vanilla soy milk

1 tablespoon agave nectar

½ teaspoon ground cinnamon

Pinch nutmeg

Vegetable oil cooking spray

12 slices whole wheat bread

1. Purée the tofu, soy milk, agave nectar, cinnamon, and nutmeg in a blender. Pour the mixture into a pie plate.
2. Coat a large skillet with cooking spray. Dip each slice of bread into the tofu mixture and cook over medium heat for about 3 minutes per side, until golden brown.

DID YOU KNOW?

Agave (ah-GAH-vay) nectar, a natural sweetener, is most often produced from the sap of blue agaves that grow in Mexico. Agaves are large, spiky plants that resemble cactus, but they are actually succulents similar to aloe vera.

PER 2-SLICE SERVING·

178 calories	10.5 g protein	313 mg sodium
2.6 g fat	28.5 g carbohydrate	109 mg calcium
0.5 g saturated fat	8.6 g sugar	2.1 mg iron
12.8% calories from fat	4.2 g fiber	0.1 mg vitamin C
0 mg cholesterol		2 mcg beta-carotene
		0.6 mg vitamin E

BLUEBERRY PANCAKES

MAKES 2 SERVINGS AND ½ CUP SYRUP ■ PREPARATION TIME: 5 minutes ■ COOK TIME: 15 minutes

This recipe is so easy, you will come back to it for every pancake occasion. Try substituting bananas, apples, or mangoes for a tasty variation.

⅔ cup all-purpose flour

¼ teaspoon salt

2 teaspoons baking powder

⅔ cup plus 1 tablespoon soy milk

½ cup fresh blueberries

Vegetable oil cooking spray

Blueberry syrup (optional):

½ cup fresh blueberries

4 tablespoons maple syrup

1. Mix the flour, salt, and baking powder in a metal bowl. Add the soy milk to dry ingredients and mix until well combined. Stir in the blueberries.

2. Spray a skillet with cooking spray and warm over medium heat.

3. Using a ⅓ cup measuring cup, pour the batter into skillet. When the top bubbles and is mostly firm, flip pancakes over, and cook for another 1 to 1½ minutes. Repeat with the rest of the batter, if you are not able to fit all four pancakes in the same skillet.

4. To make blueberry syrup, if using: In a small pot, combine the blueberries and syrup and stir occasionally over medium heat. Be sure to stir so syrup does not burn. As blueberries soften, press them down with something flat, like a spatula, until most of them mash into the syrup. Cook syrup for another minute, remove from heat, and let cool. Serve on top of the pancakes.

DID YOU KNOW?

Blueberries are full of nutrition, but low in calories. They are a great source of antioxidants. Blueberries and cranberries also contain a natural compound that stops bacteria from sticking to body surfaces, which is why they help prevent urinary tract infections.

PER SERVING (2 PANCAKES):

224 calories	7.7 g protein	835 mg sodium
2 g fat	44.6 g carbohydrate	389 mg calcium
0.3 g saturated fat	6.3 g sugar	3.4 mg iron
7.4% calories from fat	3.1 g fiber	3.9 mg vitamin C
0 mg cholesterol		13 mcg beta-carotene
		1.5 mg vitamin E

CREAMY RICE CEREAL WITH GINGERY BLUEBERRIES

MAKES FOUR 1-CUP SERVINGS ■ PREPARATION TIME: 5 minutes ■ COOK TIME: 25 minutes

The fresh ginger will not only kick-start your morning with an explosion of flavor but will also fill your kitchen with a wonderful spicy aroma.

1½ cups short-grain brown rice

1½ cups fresh blueberries

¼ cup agave nectar

½ teaspoon grated fresh ginger

1. Bring 2¾ cups of water to a boil in a medium saucepan, pour in the rice, and reduce heat to a simmer. Cook, covered, for about 45 minutes, or until all the water has been absorbed and the rice is cooked through. Add water ¼ cup at a time if it needs to cook more but the water is gone.

2. Add 2½ cups of water to the cooked rice, and bring it to a simmer over medium heat. Cook for about 10 minutes, stirring frequently to achieve a creamy consistency.

3. Combine the blueberries, agave nectar, and ginger in a small saucepan. Cook over medium heat for about 5 minutes. Serve rice cereal with a spoonful of blueberries on top.

DID YOU KNOW?

Ginger is a root and very fibrous. It's best to store it in the refrigerator. Ginger is known to have many medicinal properties including calming an upset stomach.

PER SERVING (¼ OF RECIPE):

351 calories	6.4 g protein	26 mg sodium
2.3 g fat	77.2 g carbohydrate	74 mg calcium
0.4 g saturated fat	17.7 g sugar	2.1 mg iron
5.5% calories from fat	9.1 g fiber	5.4 mg vitamin C
0 mg cholesterol		18 mcg beta-carotene
		0.4 mg vitamin E

SOY YOGURT FRUIT AND GRANOLA PARFAIT

MAKES 2 SERVINGS ■ **PREPARATION TIME: 5 minutes** ■

This wonderfully simple dish is great as a quick breakfast or an impressive and healthful dessert.

½ cup granola

¾ cup vanilla soy yogurt

½ teaspoon agave nectar

¼ teaspoon ground cardamom

¼ cup fresh, seasonal berries

2 Brazil nuts

1. Divide granola between two parfait glasses.
2. In a small bowl, mix together the yogurt, agave nectar, and cardamom. Spoon this onto the granola.
3. Top the yogurt with berries.
4. Lay Brazil nuts on a flat surface and place your knife flat on top of them. Quickly whack the flat of the knife, which will smash the Brazil nuts. Scatter on top of berries.

DID YOU KNOW?

Cardamom is part of the ginger family and adds a mild spice flavor to this dish.

PER SERVING (½ OF RECIPE):

215 calories	5.5 g protein	14 mg sodium
7.5 g fat	34.2 g carbohydrate	217 mg calcium
2.8 g saturated fat	18 g sugar	1.7 mg iron
29% calories from fat	3.5 g fiber	10.9 mg vitamin C
0 mg cholesterol		2 mcg beta-carotene
		0.8 mg vitamin E

SPICED PUMPKIN OATMEAL

MAKES 4 SERVINGS ■ PREPARATION TIME: 5 minutes ■ COOK TIME: 20 minutes

Serve this warm breakfast staple with nondairy milk. For a special treat, try pumpkin spice–flavored soy milk. Add a pinch of ground cloves for extra flavor.

Oatmeal is touted as a heart-healthy food, and rightly so. Oats have soluble fiber, the type of fiber that helps to remove cholesterol from your body.

2 cups old-fashioned rolled oats

⅓ cup raisins

¼ cup dried cranberries

1 cup canned pumpkin

2 tablespoons agave nectar

4 teaspoons ground cinnamon

½ teaspoon ground nutmeg

½ teaspoon ground ginger

½ teaspoon vanilla extract

1. Combine all ingredients with 4 cups of water in a saucepan.
2. Cook over medium heat, stirring occasionally, until the liquid is mostly absorbed and the oatmeal is creamy.

DID YOU KNOW?

Creamy or chunky? If you add oatmeal to cold water and then heat them together, the oatmeal comes out creamy. If you boil the water before adding the oatmeal, it comes out chunky.

PER SERVING (¼ OF RECIPE):

274 calories	6.5 g protein	28 mg sodium
3.1 g fat	58.4 g carbohydrate	105 mg calcium
0.6 g saturated fat	20.7 g sugar	3.6 mg iron
9.6% calories from fat	8.2 g fiber	3 mg vitamin C
0 mg cholesterol		4254 mcg beta-carotene
		1 mg vitamin E

SWEET POTATO AND BLACK BEAN BRUNCH BURRITOS WITH SALSA FRESCA

MAKES 4 SERVINGS ■ **PREPARATION TIME: 20 minutes** ■ **COOK TIME: 25 minutes**

These burritos are a perfect main dish for your next brunch. The all-in-one package is an easy way for your guests to enjoy a meal. The slight acidity of the salsa fresca perfectly complements the richness of sweet potatoes and black beans. The heat of the jalapeño used in both components of the dish can be easily altered for your taste—use more or less depending on your preference.

FOR THE SALSA FRESCA:

2 cups grape tomatoes, quartered

½ jalapeño, seeded and finely chopped

2 tablespoons finely chopped red onion

¼ cup chopped fresh cilantro

1 garlic clove, minced

1 teaspoon red wine vinegar

Sea salt to taste

Freshly ground black pepper to taste

FOR THE BURRITO:

1½ pounds sweet potatoes, peeled and cut into bite-size chunks

½ cup vegetable broth

½ teaspoon dried thyme

1 teaspoon chili powder

½ teaspoon ground cumin

1 cup canned black beans (rinsed and drained)

½ jalapeño, seeded and chopped

3 scallions, sliced

Juice of 1 lime

Sea salt to taste

Freshly ground black pepper to taste

4 (8-inch) whole wheat tortillas

Beans for breakfast?

Consider black beans on toast with salsa, a favorite in Mexico. Or baked beans, a popular breakfast in England. They are loaded with soluble fiber to cut cholesterol, along with protein, calcium, and iron.

1. Combine all ingredients for salsa fresca and set aside.
2. Place sweet potatoes in a medium stockpot and add water to cover. Bring to a boil and simmer for about 6 to 8 minutes, until sweet potatoes are tender. Drain and set aside.
3. Heat broth, thyme, chili powder, and cumin in a skillet over medium heat. Simmer for 3 minutes. Add cooked sweet potatoes, black beans, and jalapeño. Cook for about 5 minutes, stirring carefully so as to not break up potatoes and beans. Stir in scallions, lime juice, salt, and black pepper.
4. Warm tortillas by placing them one by one in a dry skillet over medium heat, turning once, for a total of about a total of 1 to 2 minutes per side. Divide sweet potato mixture evenly over all tortillas and top with about ½ cup salsa. Roll tortillas tightly and slice in half before serving.

DID YOU KNOW?

Although often called "yams," sweet potatoes are actually a different vegetable and are not related to yams. Yams are much larger in size than sweet potatoes, not as starchy, and come in many colors ranging from pale orange to bright garnet. These tubers are very hard and can be a bit difficult to chop, so be sure to have a good grip on your knife and take your time.

PER SERVING (¼ OF RECIPE):

281 calories	10 g protein	731 mg sodium
2.1 g fat	59 g carbohydrate	103 mg calcium
0.4 g saturated fat	11.6 g sugar	3.8 mg iron
6.4% calories from fat	12.8 g fiber	36.9 mg vitamin C
0 mg cholesterol		13171 mcg beta-carotene
		2.2 mg vitamin E

MARVELOUS MANGO SMOOTHIE

MAKES 4 SERVINGS ■ PREPARATION TIME: 5 minutes

2 cups plain nondairy yogurt, such as soy or rice

2 cups chopped fresh mango

1 tablespoon flaxseeds

1 tablespoon agave nectar

1. Combine all ingredients in a blender and blend until smooth and flaxseeds are ground. Add ice to the blender if you prefer a frosty cold drink.

PER SERVING (¼ OF RECIPE):		
206 calories	5.5 g protein	50 mg sodium
3.7 g fat	39.6 g carbohydrate	180 mg calcium
0.5 g saturated fat	15 g sugar	1.9 mg iron
15.7% calories from fat	2.4 g fiber	26.1 mg vitamin C
0 mg cholesterol		393 mcg beta-carotene
		1.3 mg vitamin E

PEACHY KEEN SMOOTHIE *low carb*

MAKES 4 SERVINGS ■ **PREPARATION TIME: 5 minutes**

2 cups plain soy, rice, or almond milk

1 cup chopped fresh peaches

¼ teaspoon almond extract

2 tablespoons flaxseeds

1 tablespoon agave nectar

1. Combine all ingredients in a blender and blend until smooth and the flaxseeds are ground. Add ice to the blender if you prefer a frosty cold drink.

PER SERVING (¼ OF RECIPE):

129 calories	5.6 g protein	73 mg sodium
4.3 g fat	18.4 g carbohydrate	177 mg calcium
0.5 g saturated fat	10.2 g sugar	1.9 mg iron
28.1% calories from fat	3.5 g fiber	3.5 mg vitamin C
0 mg cholesterol		76 mcg beta-carotene
		2.1 mg vitamin E

LUNCH

6

OUR MIDDAY MEAL energizes us for the rest of the day. If you're looking for something quick, you'll find many delights here to choose from. If you normally have lunch on the go or at your desk, these meals are ready to box up and reheat, as you wish.

These lunches are designed for both great taste and good health. They are rich in hearty fiber, which satisfies the appetite and trims our calorie intake, as we saw in chapter 3. Our bean and vegetable dishes are also loaded with calcium, iron, and many other nutrients.

We've kept the fat content very low, so you'll skip that after-meal slowdown that fatty meals can bring. The fact is a greasy lunch actually makes the blood more viscous. That is, it makes blood "thicker"—more like oil and less like water. This is thought to be part of the reason that meat-eaters tend to have higher blood pressure, compared with vegetarians.

These healthy lunches are completely different. Loaded with good nutrition and no cholesterol or animal fat, they are the perfect midday energy break.

UDON NOODLE SALAD

oh don't use so much ginger

A mix of Thai and Japanese, this colorful salad makes a great lunch or light supper. Think of it as a low-fat version of veggie pad thai.

20 snow peas, trimmed

1 (8-ounce) package udon noodles

3 tablespoons rice vinegar

2 tablespoons reduced-sodium soy sauce

2 teaspoons minced fresh ginger

3 garlic cloves, minced

1 teaspoon agave nectar

½ teaspoon chili paste

1½ cups seeded, chopped English cucumber

1 cup shredded carrot

1 cup chopped red bell pepper

6 scallions, sliced

1. Bring a large pot of salted water to a boil. Drop in the snow peas and cook for about 30 seconds or until bright green but still crisp. Immediately remove from the boiling water with a slotted spoon and plunge into cold water to stop the cooking. When cool, drain and pat dry with paper towels. Set aside.

2. Cook udon noodles according to package directions (you can use the same pot of boiling water as was used to blanch snow peas). Drain and rinse under cold water to stop the cooking.

3. In a small bowl, combine the vinegar, soy sauce, ginger, garlic, agave nectar, and chili paste. Stir with a whisk.

4. Toss the noodles with about half of the dressing. Place the dressed noodles on a platter. Combine the snow peas, cucumber, carrot, bell pepper, and scallions in a large bowl and toss with the remaining dressing. Top noodles with vegetables and serve.

DID YOU KNOW?

For a delicious nonfat salad topping, you can use seasoned rice vinegar or lemon juice mixed with orange juice concentrate.

PER SERVING (⅙ OF RECIPE):

162 calories	6.8 g protein	208 mg sodium
0.8 g fat	34.4 g carbohydrate	49 mg calcium
0.1 g saturated fat	4.9 g sugar	1.9 mg iron
4% calories from fat	4.9 g fiber	41.6 mg vitamin C
0 mg cholesterol		2082 mcg beta-carotene
		1 mg vitamin E

BLACK BEAN AND CORN SALAD WITH LIME

MAKES 4 SERVINGS ■ **PREPARATION TIME: 15 minutes** ■ **COOK TIME: 0 minutes**

This crowd-pleasing no-fat salad can be served as is, as a burrito filling, or as a dip with tortilla chips. Consider adding mango for an exotic summer flavor or some cilantro to kick it up a notch.

1 (15-ounce) can black beans, drained and rinsed

1 small yellow bell pepper, chopped

1 small red bell pepper, chopped

1 small tomato, chopped

1 cup frozen corn, thawed

2 scallions, chopped

1 tablespoon ohopped fresh cilantro

1 teaspoon dried oregano

1 teaspoon dried basil

½ teaspoon ground cumin

Juice of ½ lime

Kosher or sea salt to taste

Freshly ground black pepper to taste

1. Combine all ingredients in a salad bowl. Serve chilled or at room temperature.

DID YOU KNOW?

Canned foods, especially beans and soups, are often high in sodium. Look for no-added-salt brands, or, for regular brands, rinse before using.

PER SERVING (¼ OF RECIPE):

154 calories	7.8 g protein	291 mg sodium
1 g fat	30.9 g carbohydrate	73 mg calcium
0.1 g saturated fat	4.2 g sugar	2.6 mg iron
5.3% calories from fat	9.8 g fiber	65.2 mg vitamin C
0 mg cholesterol		521 mcg bota oarotene
		0.6 mg vitamin E

CAULIFLOWER AND SWEET POTATO CHOWDER

MAKES SIX 1½-CUP SERVINGS ■ **PREPARATION TIME: 20 minutes** ■ **COOK TIME: 35 minutes**

There's nothing better than soup gone chowder, with great textures and flavor. In this delicious recipe, fresh basil pairs with sweet potato and cauliflower, a delightful combo. This chowder is great year-round.

3¼ cups vegetable broth

4 large shallots, minced

½ cup chopped celery

6 cups cauliflower florets (about 1 medium head)

1 cup chopped red bell pepper

1 medium sweet potato, peeled and cut into ½-inch cubes (about 1½ cups)

1 bay leaf

1 cup unsweetened soy milk

2 tablespoons finely chopped fresh basil

Kosher salt to taste

Freshly ground black pepper to taste

1. Heat ¼ cup of the vegetable broth in a large saucepan over medium heat. Add the shallots and celery and sauté for 5 minutes. Add the remaining 3 cups broth and 1 cup water and bring to a boil. Add the cauliflower, bell pepper, sweet potato, and bay leaf and bring to a boil.

2. Reduce the heat, cover, and simmer for 20 minutes. Remove the bay leaf.

3. Add the soy milk. For a heartier consistency, purée all of the soup in batches or just half the soup. Add the basil and season with salt and black pepper.

DID YOU KNOW?

Cauliflower is at its best from December to March. Unlike broccoli and cabbage, cauliflower lacks green chlorophyll because the florets are protected by the leaves; that's why it's white.

PER SERVING (⅙ OF RECIPE):

92 calories	4.4 g protein	723 mg sodium
1.1 g fat	18.5 g carbohydrate	94 mg calcium
0.2 g saturated fat	8.6 g sugar	1.4 mg iron
9.8% calories from fat	4.2 g fiber	90.5 mg vitamin C
0 mg cholesterol		3857 mcg beta-carotene
		0.9 mg vitamin E

BLACK BEAN SOUP WITH ORANGE

MAKES FIVE 1-CUP SERVINGS ■ PREPARATION TIME: 10 minutes ■ COOK TIME: 35 minutes

Black beans and oranges are a traditional combination in Brazil. In this flavorful soup, citrus flavors contrast with the earthy, rich flavor of black beans. For best results, use pulp-free or freshly squeezed orange juice.

2¼ cups vegetable broth

3 garlic cloves, finely chopped

1¼ cups chopped red onions

1 teaspoon ground cumin

1 teaspoon dried oregano

2 (15-ounce) cans black beans, with liquid

Pinch of crushed red pepper

1 bay leaf

½ cup pulp-free orange juice

Kosher or sea salt to taste

Freshly ground black pepper to taste

¼ cup chopped fresh cilantro

1. Heat ¼ cup of the vegetable broth in a large saucepan. Add the garlic and 1 cup of the onions and cook for 5 minutes. Add the cumin and oregano and cook for 1 minute.

2. Add the beans with their liquid, the remaining 2 cups of vegetable broth, crushed red pepper, and bay leaf. Bring the soup to a boil, lower the heat and simmer, uncovered for 20 minutes, stirring occasionally. Add the orange juice, salt, and black pepper.

3. Remove the bay leaf. Purée half the bean mixture in a blender or food processor and add back to the soup. Serve each bowl garnished with cilantro and remaining red onions.

DID YOU KNOW?

Usually, it's best to drain and rinse canned beans before using in a recipe. In this dish however, the beans are used together with their liquid to add a rich consistency, with no need for a thickening agent.

PER SERVING (⅕ OF RECIPE):

198 calories	10.4 g protein	1018 mg sodium
0.9 g fat	38.5 g carbohydrate	103 mg calcium
0.1 g saturated fat	5.4 g sugar	3.4 mg iron
4% calories from fat	12.9 g fiber	12.4 mg vitamin C
0 mg cholesterol		163 mcg beta-carotene
		0.2 mg vitamin E

EDAMAME AND QUINOA SALAD

MAKES FOUR 1-CUP SERVINGS ■ **PREPARATION TIME: 15 minutes** ■ **COOK TIME: 15 minutes**

This versatile recipe combines two nutritional overachievers to make a quick, cool salad. Edamame are fresh soybeans that are sold fresh or frozen. Quinoa is a light grain cultivated in the Andes since at least 3000 BC. It cooks in less than 15 minutes.

FOR THE DRESSING:

4 tablespoons lime juice

1 tablespoon agave nectar

1½ tablespoons Dijon mustard

½ teaspoon lime zest

Sea salt to taste

Black pepper to taste

FOR THE SALAD:

1 cup quinoa, rinsed in a fine sieve

1 cup chopped red bell pepper

½ red onion, finely chopped

¼ cup finely chopped fresh mint

¼ cup finely chopped fresh parsley

2 cups frozen shelled edamame, cooked according to package directions

1. Combine the dressing ingredients and set aside.
2. Bring 2 cups water to a boil in a small saucepan. Slowly add the quinoa and bring to a boil. Lower the heat, cover, and simmer for about 15 minutes. Meanwhile, combine the bell pepper, onion, mint, parsley, and edamame. Mix well.
3. Add the quinoa and dressing to the vegetable mixture and toss well. Cover and refrigerate for 30 minutes before serving.

DID YOU KNOW?

The word *edamame* means "beans on branches," which describes how these delightful pods grow. In East Asia, it has been cultivated for centuries. Quinoa is an especially high-protein grain with 8 grams of protein per cooked cup.

PER SERVING (¼ OF RECIPE):

297 calories	15.6 g protein	309 mg sodium
7.2 g fat	44.6 g carbohydrate	111 mg calcium
0.8 g saturated fat	9.8 g sugar	5.2 mg iron
20.9% calories from fat	8.8 g fiber	63.7 mg vitamin C
0 mg cholesterol		960 mcg beta-carotene
		2.6 mg vitamin E

VERY GINGERY PEAR AND SWEET POTATO SOUP

MAKES 6 SERVINGS ■ **PREPARATION TIME: 10 minutes** ■ **COOK TIME: 30 to 35 minutes**

Sweet potatoes, packed with nutrients, vitamins, and fiber are the body of this hearty soup.

2 pounds sweet potatoes (preferably garnet yams), peeled and cubed

1½ cups peeled, chopped Bosc or red d'Anjou pears (about 2 pears)

Olive oil cooking spray

1 cup chopped onions

2 tablespoons crystallized ginger

1 teaspoon ground ginger

1 (1-inch) piece peeled fresh ginger

4 cups vegetable broth

Kosher or sea salt to taste

Freshly ground black pepper to taste

1 tablespoon fresh lime juice

¼ cup sliced scallions

1. Place the sweet potatoes and 1 cup pear in a large saucepan with water to cover. Bring to a boil, lower the heat, and simmer, covered, for about 15 to 20 minutes, until sweet potatoes and pears are soft.

2. Meanwhile, coat a large skillet with cooking spray. Add the onions and sauté for 4 minutes. Transfer the onions to a food processor. Drain the sweet potatoes and pears and add them to the food processor. Add the crystallized, ground, and fresh ginger and pureé the mixture until smooth, adding some of the broth if necessary for the mixture to process more easily.

3. Add the pureé back to the saucepan. Add the broth, salt, and black pepper. Simmer for about 15 minutes. Add the lime juice. Divide among six bowls. Top each bowl with scallions and the remaining chopped pears.

DID YOU KNOW?

Yams and sweet potatoes are two different vegetables. The true yam, popular in Latin American and Caribbean cooking, is the tuber of a tropical vine and can grow over seven feet in length.

PER SERVING (⅙ OF RECIPE):

151 calories	2.3 g protein	809 mg sodium
0.3 g fat	36.6 g carbohydrate	49 mg calcium
0.1 g saturated fat	17.5 g sugar	1.2 mg iron
1.8% calories from fat	4.8 g fiber	19.8 mg vitamin C
0 mg cholesterol		11331 mcg beta-carotene
		1.3 mg vitamin E

HOPI CORN AND CHILI STEW

MAKES 8 SERVINGS ■ **PREPARATION TIME: 30 minutes** ■ **COOK TIME: 20 minutes**

This traditional Native American dish is filling, simple to make, and festive enough to serve to company.

1½ cups vegetable broth

1 onion, chopped

3 large, dried red chile peppers, crushed or ground (such as mild New Mexico chiles), or 1 ancho chile or chile negro, crushed

3 small russet potatoes, chopped

3 carrots, chopped

2 ears corn, kernels removed from cob

1 (4-ounce) can diced green chiles

6 tomatoes, chopped

¼ teaspoon black pepper

¼ teaspoon kosher or sea salt, or to taste

2 cups cooked or canned pinto beans

2 cups vegetarian hamburger crumbles or shredded seitan (optional)

1. In a large saucepan, bring the broth to a low simmer. Add all other ingredients to the pot, and simmer for 15 minutes, until potatoes are soft.

DID YOU KNOW?

Seitan (SAY-tahn) is a popular meat substitute made of wheat gluten. It can be used in all sorts of dishes: soups, stir-fries, and even grilled!

PER SERVING (⅛ OF RECIPE):		
169 calories	7 g protein	317 mg sodium
0.9 g fat	36.3 g carbohydrate	57 mg calcium
0.2 g saturated fat	6.1 g sugar	2.9 mg iron
4.6% calories from fat	8 g fiber	32.9 mg vitamin C
0 mg cholesterol		2167 mcg beta-carotene
		1.2 mg vitamin E

FAVA BEAN AND TOMATO STEW

MAKES 4 SERVINGS ■ **PREPARATION TIME: 10 minutes** ■ **COOK TIME: 35 minutes**

This substantial stew perfumes the air with the aromas of cumin and browned garlic. If you like, lima beans can substitute for fava beans.

6 garlic cloves, minced

4¼ cups vegetable broth

4 dried New Mexico red chile peppers, ground

1 teaspoon whole cumin seeds

2 (15-ounce) cans broad beans, drained, or 4 cups cooked broad or fava beans

1 cup bulgur

1 cup fresh or frozen green peas

1 onion, chopped

4 tomatoes, chopped

½ teaspoon salt

¼ teaspoon freshly ground black pepper

Juice of 1 lemon

¼ cup chopped fresh parsley

1. In a medium saucepan, sauté garlic in ¼ cup broth over low heat until brown. Add chile peppers and cumin and sauté for 30 seconds over medium heat.
2. Add the remaining 4 cups broth, broad beans, bulgur, peas, onion, tomatoes, salt, and black pepper. Simmer for 30 minutes, until the bulgur is soft and beans are tender.
3. Remove from heat and stir in lemon juice and parsley.

DID YOU KNOW?

Tomato dishes can taste better the day after or even two or three days after they're made. Keep this stew in the refrigerator and see if you notice a difference!

PER SERVING (¼ OF RECIPE):

412 calories	20.3 g protein	1886 mg sodium
2 g fat	83.5 g carbohydrate	170 mg calcium
0.3 g saturated fat	10.8 g sugar	6.5 mg iron
4% calories from fat	25.2 g fiber	41.6 mg vitamin C
0 mg cholesterol		1157 mcg beta-carotene
		0.8 mg vitamin E

BASMATI RICE BURGERS WITH PINTO BEANS

MAKES 6 BURGERS ■ PREPARATION TIME: 60 minutes ■ COOK TIME: 10 minutes

This burger is so flavorful, even your not-yet-vegetarian friends will ask for more!

¼ cup vegetable broth

1 small onion, chopped

1 garlic clove, minced

1 teaspoon chili powder

½ teaspoon ground cumin

¼ teaspoon cayenne pepper

Kosher or sea salt to taste

Freshly ground black pepper to taste

1 cup canned pinto beans, drained and rinsed

1 cup cooked brown basmati rice

¾ cup panko bread crumbs

¼ cup finely chopped fresh parsley

Vegetable oil cooking spray

6 whole-grain hamburger buns

1 large tomato, thinly sliced

6 butter lettuce leaves

2 teaspoons whole-grain mustard or chutney of choice

1. Heat the broth in a large skillet over medium heat. Add the onion and garlic and sauté for 4 minutes. Add the chili powder, cumin, cayenne, salt, and black pepper. Add the beans and turn heat to high. Mash beans coarsely as they cook over high heat for about 2 minutes, being careful to not let the beans burn.

2. Transfer the beans into a bowl. Add the rice, bread crumbs, and parsley, and stir until combined. Form into six patties, place them on a plate, and let rest in the refrigerator for 30 minutes.

3. Heat a large skillet, preferably cast-iron, over medium heat and coat it with cooking spray. Place the patties in the skillet (in batches if necessary, being sure to spray the pan with cooking spray in between each batch) and cook for about 4 minutes per side, until brown and heated through. Serve on buns with tomato, lettuce, and mustard.

DID YOU KNOW?

Raw pinto beans are beige with splashes of reddish-brown color, which is why they are called *pinto*—that's "painted" in Spanish. When cooked, the colored patches fade away, leaving the pink-beige bean we all know.

PER BURGER:

280 calories	12.4 g protein	638 mg sodium
3.5 g fat	50.6 g carbohydrate	111 mg calcium
0.7 g saturated fat	7 g sugar	3.2 mg iron
10.8% calories from fat	9 g fiber	8.9 mg vitamin C
0 mg cholesterol		506 mcg beta-carotene
		0.9 mg vitamin E

CAJUN BEAN SOUP

MAKES SIX 1-CUP SERVINGS ■ **PREPARATION TIME: 10 minutes** ■ **COOK TIME: 20 minutes**

Puréeing this soup melds its flavors. If you are running short on time, feel free to leave it as is. It's delicious either way.

4 slices low-fat vegetarian bacon (optional)

4¼ cups vegetable broth

4 small carrots, thinly sliced

1 medium onion, chopped

3 garlic cloves, minced

½ teaspoon dried oregano

½ teaspoon dried basil

½ teaspoon dried thyme

¼ teaspoon crushed red pepper, or a few drops Tabasco sauce

Kosher or sea salt to taste

Black pepper to taste

2 (15-ounce) cans great Northern beans, with liquid

2 cups chopped fresh spinach

1. Cook vegetarian bacon, if using, in a nonstick skillet over medium-high heat until crisp. Set aside.

2. In a large saucepan, heat ¼ cup broth. Add the carrots, onion, and garlic and sauté for 5 minutes. Add the remaining 4 cups broth, oregano, basil, thyme, crushed red pepper, salt, black pepper, and beans and their liquid. Bring to a boil, reduce heat to low, and simmer for 5 minutes.

3. Purée soup in batches, if necessary, in a food processor or blender. Return to pot. Add spinach. Crumble bacon, if using, and stir into the soup.

DID YOU KNOW?

Many people think of Cajun food as hot and spicy. But true Cajun food has just a bit of a kick; it won't drive you to tears.

PER SERVING (⅙ OF RECIPE):

169 calories	9.5 g protein	1021 mg sodium
0.8 g fat	32.8 g carbohydrate	80 mg calcium
0.2 g saturated fat	4.4 g sugar	2.7 mg iron
3.8% calories from fat	10.2 g fiber	4.3 mg vitamin C
0 mg cholesterol		3284 mcg beta-carotene
		1.5 mg vitamin E

QUINOA AND CARROT SALAD

MAKES 4 SERVINGS ■ PREPARATION TIME: 15 minutes ■ COOK TIME: 15 minutes

This light, spicy-sweet salad will tease your taste buds. Try adding any leftover beets, broccoli, or other vegetables you have on hand.

1 cup quinoa

1½ pounds carrots, thinly sliced

Juice of 1½ lemons

1½ teaspoons agave nectar

1 garlic clove, minced

¾ teaspoon ground cinnamon

¼ teaspoon ground cumin

3 pinches of cayenne pepper

Kosher or sea salt to taste

Freshly ground black pepper to taste

½ cup golden raisins

1. Rinse quinoa in a fine sieve under running water for about 1 minute. Bring 2 cups water to a boil in a medium saucepan. Pour in the quinoa and return to a boil. Lower heat, cover, and simmer for 15 minutes.

2. Meanwhile, bring 2 quarts water to a boil in a large saucepan. Drop in the carrots and cook for 2 minutes. Drain and set aside.

3. In a large bowl, whisk the lemon juice, agave nectar, garlic, cinnamon, cumin, cayenne, salt, and black pepper. Add the quinoa, carrots, and raisins. Toss. Refrigerate for 1 hour. Serve chilled or at room temperature.

DID YOU KNOW?

Although most commonly orange, carrots come in a variety of colors, including white, black, purple, and yellow.

PER SERVING (¼ OF RECIPE):		
273 calories	7.8 g protein	240 mg sodium
3 g fat	56.6 g carbohydrate	88 mg calcium
0.4 g saturated fat	19.6 g sugar	3.1 mg iron
9.8% calories from fat	8.2 g fiber	8.6 mg vitamin C
0 mg cholesterol		11628 mcg beta-carotene
		2.5 mg vitamin E

TEMPEH BURGERS WITH PINEAPPLE SALSA

MAKES 4 BURGERS ■ PREPARATION TIME: 15 minutes plus 1 hour to marinate ■ COOK TIME: 10 minutes

For a tropical twist on veggie burgers, add this tangy fruit salsa.

FOR THE MARINADE:

6 tablespoons tamari

4 tablespoons mirin

2 tablespoons grated fresh ginger

4 garlic cloves, minced

1 teaspoon orange zest

1 (8-ounce) package tempeh, cut into 4 pieces

FOR THE SALSA:

2 cups chopped fresh pineapple

½ cup chopped fresh or frozen mango

3 tablespoons finely chopped red onion

3 tablespoons finely chopped red bell pepper

2 scallions, finely chopped

1 tablespoon fresh lime juice

1 teaspoon agave nectar, or to taste

2 pinches of cayenne pepper

Vegetable oil cooking spray

4 whole-grain hamburger buns

1. Combine the tamari, mirin, ginger, garlic, and orange zest in a shallow bowl. Place the tempeh into the bowl and marinate in the refrigerator for 1 hour, turning halfway through.

2. Meanwhile combine all salsa ingredients, cover, and refrigerate until serving time.

3. Heat a heavy skillet (preferably cast-iron) over medium-high heat. Coat with cooking spray. Add the tempeh, with marinade, and sear tempeh for about 4 minutes per side.

4. Place the tempeh slices on whole-grain buns. Top with salsa.

DID YOU KNOW?

Because it symbolizes hospitality, the pineapple is a common motif in carved doors, gates, and entryways.

PER BURGER:

328 calories	18.7 g protein	1562 mg sodium
7.8 g fat	46.2 g carbohydrate	146 mg calcium
1.6 g saturated fat	19.6 g sugar	3.7 mg iron
20.3% calories from fat	7.2 g fiber	58.8 mg vitamin C
0 mg cholesterol		305 mcg beta-carotene
		0.9 mg vitamin E

TEMPEH SLOPPY JOES

MAKES 4 SERVINGS ■ **PREPARATION TIME: 10 minutes** ■ **COOK TIME: 20 minutes**

Everyone needs a good Sloppy Joe recipe. You will love every bite of these.

1 small onion, chopped

1 green bell pepper, seeded and chopped

1 (8-ounce) package tempeh, crumbled into small pieces

1 (8-ounce) can tomato sauce

2 tablespoons ketchup

1 tablespoon agave nectar

1 tablespoon apple cider vinegar

1 tablespoon vegan Worcestershire sauce

2 teaspoons prepared mustard

½ teaspoon garlic powder

4 multigrain hamburger buns

1. Heat ½ cup water in a skillet. Add the onion and bell pepper and sauté until cooked through. Add remaining ½ cup water and tempeh. Sauté for 5 to 7 minutes, allowing the tempeh to become well-done.

2. Add the tomato sauce, ketchup, agave nectar, vinegar, Worcestershire sauce, mustard, and garlic powder and cook for 15 minutes.

3. Serve on buns.

DID YOU KNOW?

You can substitute faux meat crumbles, textured vegetable protein (TVP), or even lentils in this recipe.

PER SERVING:

273 calories	17.6 g protein	666 mg sodium
7.9 g fat	36.6 g carbohydrate	143 mg calcium
1.6 g saturated fat	14.4 g sugar	3.9 mg iron
24.5% calories from fat	6.3 g fiber	27.7 mg vitamin C
0 mg cholesterol		239 mcg beta-carotene
		1.5 mg vitamin E

BLACK BEAN TARTINES

MAKES 4 SERVINGS ■ PREPARATION TIME: 15 minutes ■ COOK TIME: 0 minutes

This dish is sure to please. It is meant to be served as an open-faced sandwich, but without the bread it makes a tasty dip for baked tortilla chips.

1 (15-ounce) can black beans, drained and rinsed

2 tablespoons tomato juice

2 tablespoons fresh lime juice

2 garlic cloves, minced

1 small jalapeño pepper, seeded and minced

Kosher or sea salt to taste

Freshly ground black pepper to taste

4 slices pumpernickel bread

1 avocado, thinly sliced

1 small tomato, finely chopped

3 tablespoons finely chopped red onion

1. Put the beans, tomato juice, lime juice, garlic, jalapeño pepper, salt, and black pepper into a food processor or blender and purée until well mixed, but still chunky.

2. Equally divide the purée among bread slices. Top each tartine with avocado, tomato, and onion. Serve open-faced with a fork and knife or cut the tartines into squares and eat them with your hands.

DID YOU KNOW?

Black beans are rich in antioxidants. These humble legumes contain over 4,000 antioxidants, more than any other variety of beans. And beans are also rich in healthy fiber, leaving you feeling full and satisfied.

PER SERVING (¼ OF RECIPE):

238 calories	9.3 g protein	484 mg sodium
6.7 g fat	37.5 g carbohydrate	83 mg calcium
1 g saturated fat	2.7 g sugar	2.9 mg iron
23.4% calories from fat	11.7 g fiber	12.1 mg vitamin C
0 mg cholesterol		158 mcg beta-carotene
		1 mg vitamin E

CREAM OF ASPARAGUS SOUP *low carb*

MAKES FOUR 1-CUP SERVINGS ■ **PREPARATION TIME: 5 minutes** ■ **COOK TIME: 35 minutes**

When Robyn's mother, who has had diabetes for forty-four years, decided to go vegan about twenty years ago, one of the "food issues" she had to resolve was her love of creamy soups. After experimenting with all sorts of healthful diabetes-friendly recipes, she has found her staple soup. Her first comment was, "I can't have this, there is cream in here!" One look at the printed recipe shows otherwise.

3 cups sliced asparagus (about 1 pound)

2 cups vegetable broth (use 1½ cups for a thicker soup)

¾ teaspoon chopped fresh thyme

1 bay leaf

1 garlic clove, crushed

2 tablespoons whole wheat pastry flour

2 cups plain soy milk

Pinch of ground nutmeg

1 teaspoon salt

¼ teaspoon grated lemon zest

½ tablespoon lemon juice

Freshly ground black pepper to taste

Hot sauce to taste

1. Combine asparagus, broth, ½ teaspoon thyme, bay leaf, and garlic in a large saucepan over medium-high heat. Bring to a boil. Cover, reduce heat, and simmer for 10 minutes. Discard the bay leaf. Place the asparagus mixture in a blender, cover, and purée until smooth.

2. Place the flour in a large saucepan over medium heat. Gradually add the soy milk, stirring with a whisk until blended. Add the puréed asparagus mixture and nutmeg and stir to combine. Bring to a boil. Reduce heat and simmer for 5 minutes. Remove from heat and strain. Add the remaining ¼ teaspoon thyme, salt, lemon zest, lemon juice, and black pepper. Add hot sauce to taste.

DID YOU KNOW?

Asparagus is a nutritional powerhouse, packed with fiber and folate that promotes heart health.

PER SERVING (¼ OF RECIPE):

108 calories	7.1 g protein	1159 mg sodium
2.3 g fat	17.1 g carbohydrate	179 mg calcium
0.4 g saturated fat	6 g sugar	2.3 mg iron
17.9% calories from fat	3.8 g fiber	9.2 mg vitamin C
0 mg cholesterol		691 mcg beta-carotene
		3.2 mg vitamin E

LEMONY LENTIL VEGETABLE STEW

MAKES FIVE 1-CUP SERVINGS ■ **PREPARATION TIME: 10 minutes** ■ **COOK TIME: 35 minutes**

These earthy, sweet flavors will awaken your taste buds in the middle of a cold winter.

1 teaspoon whole peppercorns

1 sprig fresh rosemary

4¼ cups vegetable broth

2 tablespoons lemon juice

1 cup dried lentils

1 medium sweet potato, peeled and cubed (about 1½ cups)

1 cup cubed baby eggplant (no need to peel)

1 onion, chopped

2 garlic cloves, sliced

1 cup sliced baby carrots

½ teaspoon sea salt

1. Put peppercorns and the rosemary sprig into a cheesecloth and tie the corners.
2. In a large saucepan, bring 4 cups broth, lemon juice, and the cheesecloth package to a boil.
3. Add the lentils, sweet potato, and eggplant. Reduce heat, cover, and cook for 20 minutes.
4. Meanwhile, in a nonstick skillet, heat remaining ¼ cup broth, then add the onion and garlic and cook for 3 minutes.
5. Add carrots, 1 tablespoon water, and salt and cook for 6 minutes. If you want your carrots completely soft, add about 4 minutes to the cooking time.
6. Once lentils, sweet potato, and eggplant have been cooking for 20 minutes, remove the cheesecloth with peppercorns and rosemary, and add vegetable mixture. Cover and cook for 5 more minutes.

DID YOU KNOW?

Lentils come in their own rainbow of colors: red, orange, yellow, green, and black.

PER SERVING (⅕ OF RECIPE):

250 calories	8.7 g protein	1392 mg sodium
2.4 g fat	52.3 g carbohydrate	80 mg calcium
0.3 g saturated fat	22.4 g sugar	3.3 mg iron
8.1% calories from fat	8.2 g fiber	27.5 mg vitamin C
0 mg cholesterol		1746 mcg beta-carotene
		1.4 mg vitamin E

SPICY GALA APPLE, CHICKPEA, AND MANGO CHUTNEY SOUP

MAKES 4 SERVINGS ■ PREPARATION TIME: 15 minutes ■ COOK TIME: 20 minutes

This wonderful soup combines Indian spices with the sweetness of apples and mango.

4 cups vegetable broth

2 Gala apples, peeled and chopped

¾ cup chopped onion

½ cup chopped carrot

½ cup chopped celery

½ cup chopped green bell pepper

2 tablespoons whole wheat pastry flour

1½ teaspoons curry powder

1 teaspoon ground ginger

Crushed red pepper to taste

Kosher or sea salt to taste

Freshly ground black pepper to taste

1 (15-ounce) can chickpeas, drained

⅓ cup mango chutney

2 tablespoons tomato paste

1. Heat ¼ cup broth in a large pot over medium-high heat.
2. Add the apples, onion, carrot, celery, and bell pepper. Cook for 5 minutes. Stir in flour, curry powder, ginger, crushed red pepper, salt, and black pepper and cook for 1 minute. Stir in remaining 3¾ cups broth, chickpeas, chutney, and tomato paste. Bring to a boil.
3. Reduce heat and simmer for 8 minutes.

DID YOU KNOW?

Gala apples are good for eating and baking. Most Galas are yellow with red stripes, although some varieties are now solidly red.

PER SERVING (¼ OF RECIPE):

250 calories	8.7 g protein	1333 mg sodium
2.4 g fat	52.1 g carbohydrate	80 mg calcium
0.3 g saturated fat	22.2 g sugar	3.3 mg iron
8.1% calories from fat	8.2 g fiber	27.5 mg vitamin C
0 mg cholesterol		1731 mcg beta-carotene
		1.4 mg vitamin E

WHITE BEAN AND TOMATO SALAD

MAKES FOUR 1-CUP SERVINGS ■ **PREPARATION TIME: 20 minutes** ■ **COOK TIME: 0 minutes**

Fresh basil makes this salad a colorful treat—your eyes will enjoy it almost as much as your taste buds! This recipe will soon become one of your summertime favorites.

2 (15-ounce) cans white beans, drained and rinsed

2 medium tomatoes, seeded and chopped

¼ cup chopped red onion

½ cup finely chopped fresh parsley

¼ cup chopped fresh basil

2 tablespoons white wine vinegar

2 teaspoons lemon zest

½ teaspoon Dijon mustard

Kosher or sea salt to taste

Black pepper to taste

1. Combine the beans, tomatoes, onion, parsley, and basil in a salad bowl.
2. In a separate small bowl, whisk together the vinegar, lemon zest, and mustard. Season with salt and black pepper. Add to salad and toss. Serve chilled or at room temperature.

DID YOU KNOW?

Red tomatoes are high in lycopene—an antioxidant that helps prevent cancer and heart disease.

PER SERVING (¼ OF RECIPE):

222 calories	15.1 g protein	398 mg sodium
0.8 g fat	40.5 g carbohydrate	156 mg calcium
0.2 g saturated fat	2.9 g sugar	6.2 mg iron
2.9% calories from fat	10.5 g fiber	20.4 mg vitamin C
0 mg cholesterol		742 mcg beta-carotene
		1.8 mg vitamin E

CHICKPEA PATTIES WITH MANGO CHUTNEY

MAKES 4 SANDWICHES ■ PREPARATION TIME: 25 minutes ■ COOK TIME: 30 minutes

Indian spices make these chickpea patties burst with flavor. Add mango chutney for a bit of a spice and texture.

¼ cup vegetable broth

1 small onion, chopped

3 tablespoons finely chopped celery

2 tablespoons finely chopped red bell pepper

2 tablespoons finely chopped fresh parsley

2 garlic cloves, minced

2 teaspoons curry powder

¼ teaspoon ground cumin

Pinch of cayenne pepper

Kosher or sea salt to taste

Freshly ground black pepper to taste

2 cups canned chickpeas (drained and rinsed)

1½ cups panko bread crumbs

Vegetable oil cooking spray

4 whole-grain buns, toasted

½ cup mango chutney

8 tomato slices

4 lettuce leaves

1. Heat the broth in a medium skillet over medium heat. Add the onion and sauté for 3 minutes. Add the celery, bell pepper, parsley, and garlic and sauté for 2 minutes. Add the curry powder, cumin, cayenne, salt, and black pepper and remove from heat.

2. Purée chickpeas in a food processor or blender, adding a little water if necessary. Pulse until you have a coarse purée. Place chickpeas in a large bowl. Add vegetable mixture and bread crumbs and mix well.

3. Form the mixture into four patties. Heat a heavy skillet (preferably cast-iron) over medium-high heat. If you are using a regular skillet, coat with cooking spray. Add patties and brown on both sides for about 5 to 6 minutes per side.

4. Place patties on toasted buns and top with mango chutney, tomato, and lettuce.

DID YOU KNOW?

Chickpeas are part of the legume family. They are grown in subtropical climates and contain 2 or 3 peas per pod.

PER SANDWICH:

475 calories	19.7 g protein	859 mg sodium
6.1 g fat	87 g carbohydrate	196 mg calcium
1.1 g saturated fat	20.6 g sugar	6.5 mg iron
11.2% calories from fat	11.6 g fiber	25.9 mg vitamin C
0 mg cholesterol		507 mcg beta-carotene
		1.3 mg vitamin E

SUMMER PASTA AND BEAN SALAD WITH FRESH TOMATOES AND BASIL

MAKES SIX 1½-CUP SERVINGS ■ PREPARATION TIME: 10 minutes ■ COOK TIME: 40 minutes

With fresh basil and tomatoes, this is a great dish to share at picnics or potlucks.

1 (8-ounce) package whole wheat rotini or other shaped pasta

2 large tomatoes, chopped

½ red onion, thinly sliced

3 scallions, thinly sliced

½ cup chopped fresh basil

1 (15-ounce) can white beans, drained and rinsed

1 teaspoon dried oregano

2 tablespoons balsamic vinegar

Kosher or sea salt to taste

Freshly ground black pepper to taste

1. Cook pasta according to package directions. Drain and rinse.
2. Combine pasta with remaining ingredients and let stand for 30 minutes at room temperature prior to serving.

DID YOU KNOW?

Basil is easy to grow in your home, garden, or apartment window box. You will want to find out when it is best to plant basil depending on where you live. With adequate sunshine, you will have enough to add to every smoothie, meal, or snack within a few short weeks.

PER SERVING (⅙ OF RECIPE):

219 calories	11.2 g protein	232 mg sodium
0.9 g fat	44.7 g carbohydrate	84 mg calcium
0.2 g saturated fat	4.1 g sugar	3.4 mg iron
3.5% calories from fat	7.2 g fiber	10.5 mg vitamin C
0 mg cholesterol		437 mcg beta-carotene
		1.2 mg vitamin E

MINTY BLACK BEAN, JICAMA, AND CUCUMBER SALAD

MAKES SIX 1-CUP SERVINGS ■ **PREPARATION TIME: 5 minutes** ■ **COOK TIME: 0 minutes**

The rice vinegar dressing in this recipe brings all the flavors to your palate in the most light and refreshing way. Fresh mint is best in this recipe, but if you can't find it, cilantro is great as well. For more variations, consider adding mango, or substituting chickpeas for black beans. In this recipe, anything goes!

1 medium jicama, peeled and chopped

1 large cucumber, peeled, seeded, and chopped

1 medium red onion, halved and thinly sliced

1 (15-ounce) can black beans, drained and rinsed

2 tablespoons finely chopped fresh mint

¼ cup rice vinegar

Sea salt to taste

Freshly ground black pepper to taste

1. Combine all ingredients, cover, and refrigerate several hours to combine the flavors.

DID YOU KNOW?

Jicama is a root vegetable, but be sure not to mistake it for a rutabaga or turnip. It has a brown textured skin and just needs to be peeled and chopped, not cooked first, and it chops easier than a potato. You will find jicama in most grocery stores and at any Latin specialty markets.

PER SERVING (⅙ OF RECIPE):

125 calories	5.3 g protein	246 mg sodium
0.5 g fat	25.2 g carbohydrate	62 mg calcium
0.1 g saturated fat	1.7 g sugar	2.2 mg iron
3.4% calories from fat	11.3 g fiber	25.8 mg vitamin C
0 mg cholesterol		50 mcg beta-carotene
		0.6 mg vitamin E

HUMMUS PIZZA

MAKES 4 PIZZAS ■ **PREPARATION TIME: 5 minutes** ■ **COOK TIME: 15 minutes**

Hummus is so easy to prepare at home, you'll wonder why anyone buys commercial versions. And at home, you control the fat and calories. Sesame seed butter, called tahini, brings a thick consistency and savory flavor. This recipe turns hummus from a snack into a meal.

1 (15-ounce) can chickpeas, drained

3 garlic cloves, minced

2½ tablespoons fresh lemon juice

1 tablespoon tahini

¼ teaspoon salt

¼ teaspoon freshly ground black pepper

4 whole wheat pita breads

¼ cup soy Parmesan cheese

1 small tomato, chopped

1 teaspoon dried oregano

1. Preheat the oven to 375°F.
2. In a blender or food processor, combine the chickpeas, garlic, lemon juice, tahini, salt, and black pepper. Blend until smooth.
3. Spread chickpea mixture over the four pita breads. Place all breads on a baking sheet. Sprinkle each pita bread with soy cheese, tomato, and oregano. Bake for 6 to 8 minutes, until cheese is lightly browned and bread is toasted.

DID YOU KNOW?

A serving of beans will fill you up more than most foods, thanks to our friend, fiber. Fiber also helps control blood sugar, providing a steady supply of energy.

PER PIZZA:

286 calories	13.4 g protein	568 mg sodium
6.2 g fat	48 g carbohydrate	76 mg calcium
0.8 g saturated fat	4.9 g sugar	4.2 mg iron
18.1% calories from fat	8.6 g fiber	8.8 mg vitamin C
0 mg cholesterol		84 mcg beta-carotene
		0.8 mg vitamin E

RED AND WHITE QUINOA PILAF

MAKES SIX ½-CUP SERVINGS ■ **PREPARATION TIME: 15 minutes** ■ **COOK TIME: 20 minutes**

This is a clean, fresh dish and a great introduction to quinoa, a high-protein grain.

⅓ cup raisins

Vegetable oil cooking spray

½ cup chopped onion

2 teaspoons minced fresh ginger

2 garlic cloves, minced

½ cup quinoa

½ cup red quinoa

2 cups vegetable broth

1 cup drained canned chickpeas

2 tablespoons finely chopped fresh mint

2 tablespoons lime juice

Sea salt to taste

Freshly ground black pepper to taste

1. Immerse raisins in hot water for 10 minutes. Drain and set aside.
2. Coat a large skillet with cooking spray. Add the onion, ginger, and garlic and sauté for 4 minutes. Add both quinoas and sauté 1 minute.
3. Add broth and bring to a boil. Lower heat, cover, and cook for 15 minutes. Fluff quinoa with a fork and add raisins, chickpeas, mint, and lime juice. Cook for 1 minute. Season with salt and black pepper.

DID YOU KNOW?

The Incas referred to quinoa as *chisaya mama*, or "mother of all grains," holding the crop to be sacred.

PER SERVING (⅙ OF RECIPE):

186 calories	7 g protein	505 mg sodium
2.5 g fat	35.2 g carbohydrate	44 mg calcium
0.3 g saturated fat	8.2 g sugar	2.6 mg iron
12% calories from fat	4.4 g fiber	3.1 mg vitamin C
0 mg cholesterol		109 mcg beta-carotene
		0.9 mg vitamin E

-less red pepper flakes

WILD RICE PILAF WITH ROASTED GARLIC AND SPINACH

MAKES FOUR 1-CUP SERVINGS ■ **PREPARATION TIME: 5 minutes** ■ **COOK TIME: 1 hour 10 minutes**

Wild rice, a traditional Native American grain, offers this pilaf a nutty flavor and delightful texture.

2 garlic bulbs

2½ cups vegetable broth

2 teaspoons paprika (preferably smoked paprika)

½ teaspoon black pepper

¼ teaspoon crushed red pepper

1 cup brown Arborio rice

¼ cup wild rice

2 pounds fresh spinach

Kosher or sea salt to taste

1. Preheat oven to 425°F.
2. Cut the tops off the garlic bulbs, dunk bulbs in water, and cover in foil. Place in a small baking dish and bake for 35 minutes.
3. In a medium saucepan, combine the broth, paprika, black pepper, and crushed red pepper. Bring to a boil. Stir in brown and wild rice and bring to a boil. Cover and reduce heat to low. Cook for 50 to 60 minutes or until the rice is tender and the broth is fully absorbed.
4. While the rice is cooking, wash the spinach thoroughly and chop. Set aside.
5. When the garlic is done, allow to cool slightly, and squeeze out the garlic cloves. Mash with a fork.
6. Once rice is cooked, stir in spinach and roasted garlic. Season with salt.

DID YOU KNOW?

Do you love garlic? In addition to serving as a flavor boost for many recipes, garlic is also nutritious. It is a member of the allium family, which is under investigation for possible anticancer effects.

PER SERVING (¼ OF RECIPE):

278 calories	10.9 g protein	845 mg sodium
2.1 g fat	57 g carbohydrate	240 mg calcium
0.4 g saturated fat	4.2 g sugar	6.5 mg iron
6.4% calories from fat	10 g fiber	19.3 mg vitamin C
0 mg cholesterol		9213 mcg beta-carotene
		3.4 mg vitamin E

BLACK BEAN CAKES WITH MANGO SALSA

MAKES 4 SERVINGS ■ **PREPARATION TIME: 30 minutes** ■ **COOK TIME: 30 minutes**

This dish is bright, delicious, and versatile. You can serve the cakes as big-mouth burger patties or bite-size appetizers.

FOR THE BEAN CAKES:

½ cup hot or mild salsa

2 teaspoons ground cumin

2 (15-ounce) cans black beans, drained

1½ cups bread crumbs

¼ cup finely chopped scallions

Kosher or sea salt to taste

Black pepper to taste

Vegetable oil cooking spray

FOR THE SALSA:

2 ripe mangoes, peeled and cubed

¼ cup finely chopped red onion

¼ cup finely chopped red bell pepper

2 tablespoons finely chopped scallions

2 tablespoons finely chopped fresh cilantro

2 tablespoons fresh lime juice

2 teaspoons sugar or agave nectar

Pinch of cayenne pepper

1. Preheat the oven to 200°F. Combine the salsa, cumin, and black beans in a food processor and pulse until smooth. Add 1 cup bread crumbs, scallions, salt, and black pepper.

2. Divide the mixture into small patties, roughly ⅛ cup each. Dredge the patties in the remaining ½ cup bread crumbs. Set the patties on a tray and refrigerate for 30 minutes.

3. While the bean cakes chill, combine all salsa ingredients and refrigerate until serving time.

4. Heat a nonstick large skillet over medium heat. Using cooking spray throughout the sauté process, sauté the cakes for about 3 minutes per side, watching carefully so the cakes don't burn. Place the cakes on a baking sheet and place in the 200°F oven until all cakes are prepared. Serve the cakes with the salsa.

DID YOU KNOW?

Cayenne contains a pungent resinlike substance known as capsaicin, which is used topically as a pain reliever.

PER SERVING (¼ OF RECIPE):

462 calories	18.9 g protein	1200 mg sodium
3.7 g fat	91.7 g carbohydrate	213 mg calcium
0.7 g saturated fat	20.7 g sugar	6.5 mg iron
6.9% calories from fat	20.2 g fiber	47.9 mg vitamin C
0 mg cholesterol		759 mcg beta-carotene
		1.9 mg vitamin E

FRENCH COUNTRY STEW

so good

MAKES FOUR 1-CUP SERVINGS ■ **PREPARATION TIME: 10 minutes** ■ **COOK TIME: 45 minutes**

The ease of preparation of this stew is only surpassed by its wonderful marriage of winter vegetables and flavors. Perfect for a family night, a warm dinner after a snow day, or a week of wonderful lunches at work. To make it even easier, look for prepeeled and cubed squash in your supermarket.

4¼ cups vegetable broth

1 large onion, chopped

2 garlic cloves, minced

3 cups peeled and cubed butternut squash

3 cups coarsely chopped green cabbage

1 tablespoon chopped fresh thyme

¼ teaspoon crushed red pepper

1 (16-ounce) can white beans, drained and rinsed

1 cup canned diced tomatoes

Kosher or sea salt to taste

Freshly ground black pepper to taste

1. Heat ¼ cup broth in a large saucepan over medium heat. Add the onion and garlic and sauté for 5 minutes. Add the squash, cabbage, remaining 4 cups broth, thyme, and crushed red pepper and bring to boil.
2. Lower heat, cover, and simmer on medium-low for about 30 minutes, or until the squash is tender.
3. Add the beans and tomatoes, cover, and continue to simmer for 10 minutes. Season with salt and black pepper.

DID YOU KNOW?

Butternut squash also makes really great French fries! Preheat your oven to 425°F. Sprinkle the squash (peeled and cut into French-fry shapes) with salt and pepper or a combination of your favorite spices (paprika, cumin, or coriander work great). Arrange the squash in one layer, allowing space between individual pieces, on a nonstick cookie sheet. Bake in the oven for about 45 minutes, turning the squash halfway through, until the inside is tender and the outside has a beautiful golden brown color.

PER SERVING (¼ OF RECIPE):

212 calories	11.2 g protein	1381 mg sodium
0.6 g fat	44.4 g carbohydrate	181 mg calcium
0.1 g saturated fat	11.4 g sugar	4.9 mg iron
2.4% calories from fat	9.1 g fiber	42.6 mg vitamin C
0 mg cholesterol		4519 mcg beta-carotene
		2.5 mg vitamin E

BERRY BARLEY SOUP

MAKES 4 SERVINGS ■ PREPARATION TIME: 5 minutes ■ COOK TIME: 30 minutes

1 cup soy creamer

2 cups plain soy milk

½ cup barley

Pinch of salt

1 sprig fresh rosemary

Zest of 1 lemon

¼ cup fresh raspberries

1. Heat the soy creamer and soy milk in a small saucepan until boiling. Stir in the barley, salt, and rosemary. Return mixture to a boil, cover, and reduce heat to low. Cook covered for 25 to 30 minutes. Be careful not to overcook the barley, or it will be mushy.

2. Remove saucepan from heat. Remove rosemary and stir in lemon zest. Allow soup to cool until it is just below room temperature. Garnish with raspberries.

PER SERVING (¼ OF RECIPE):

221 calories	8.4 g protein	165 mg sodium
4.5 g fat	37.7 g carbohydrate	173 mg calcium
0.6 g saturated fat	7.1 g sugar	2.3 mg iron
18.6% calories from fat	7 g fiber	3.4 mg vitamin C
0 mg cholesterol		7 mcg beta-carotene
		2.1 mg vitamin E

▶ **All-American Scramble on Pumpernickel Bagel** (Page 60)

▶ **Vanilla French Toast** (page 61) **and Grilled Peaches with Sweet Balsamic Glaze** (page179)

▶ **Chocolate Cherry Nirvana** (page 168) **and Creamy Fruit Smoothie** (page 164)

Udon Noodle Salad (page 72)

▶ **Very Gingery Pear and Sweet Potato Soup** (page 77)

▶ **Spinach, Beet, and Orange Salad with Ginger-Agave Dressing** (page 176)

▶ **Italian Fusilli with Sun-dried Tomatoes and Artichoke Hearts** (page 106)

▶ **Curry Popcorn** (page 166) **and Italian Chickpea Nibbles** (page 169)

▶ **Sun-dried Tomato Spread** (page 162), **Curried Chickpea Spread** (page 159), **and Spinach Dip** (page163)

▶ **Black Bean Cakes with Mango Salsa** (page 96)

▶ **Saffron Risotto with Peas and Asparagus** (page 189)

► **Strawberries in Marsala** (page 191)

FIRE-ROASTED TOMATO BLACK BEAN CHILI

MAKES 6 SERVINGS ■ **PREPARATION TIME: 20 minutes** ■ **COOK TIME: 20 minutes**

½ yellow onion, sliced

6 garlic cloves, minced

1 (15-ounce) can fire-roasted tomatoes

Juice of 1 lime

2 tablespoons finely chopped fresh cilantro

2 (15-ounce) cans black beans, with liquid

2 teaspoons ground cumin

3 tablespoons chili powder

2 tablespoons chipotle powder

2 teaspoons dried Mexican oregano

2 teaspoons salt

½ cup TVP crumbles (optional)

1. In a large saucepan on high heat, sauté the onion in ¼ cup water until it starts to turn brown.
2. Add ¼ cup water and stir. Add garlic and cook for three minutes.
3. Add the tomatoes, lime juice, cilantro, beans and their liquid, cumin, chili powders, oregano, salt, and TVP crumbles, if using.
4. Reduce heat to medium and cook for 10 minutes.

PER SERVING (⅙ OF RECIPE):		
177 calories	9.6 g protein	1302 mg sodium
1.6 g fat	34 g carbohydrate	121 mg calcium
0.3 g saturated fat	3.7 g sugar	4.3 mg iron
7.5% calories from fat	12.7 g fiber	13 mg vitamin C
0 mg cholesterol		850 mcg beta-carotene
		1.8 mg vitamin E

WINTER VEGETABLE POTAGE *low carb*

MAKES EIGHT 1-CUP SERVINGS ■ PREPARATION TIME: 30 minutes ■ COOK TIME: 40 minutes

Potage is a French word meaning a thick, hearty soup and this recipe makes use of root vegetables that are available all winter. I (Robyn) was first introduced to potage in an old French country house where our affable hosts had a pot of this stewing practically every day.

5½ cups vegetable broth

1½ cups chopped onions

1 cup chopped carrots

1 cup finely chopped fennel

Kosher salt to taste

1 cup sliced green cabbage

1 medium sweet potato, peeled and chopped (about 1½ cups)

½ cup peeled chopped rutabaga

Black pepper to taste

1 cup chopped broccoli

2 tablespoons minced fresh chives, for garnish

1. Heat ½ cup broth in a large saucepan over medium high-heat. Add the onions, carrots, and fennel. Season with salt and sauté for 7 to 8 minutes.

2. Add the remaining 5 cups broth, cabbage, sweet potatoes, and rutabaga and season with more salt, if necessary, and black pepper. Bring to a boil. Cover pot and simmer on low for 15 minutes or until vegetables are tender. Add broccoli and cook for 5 more minutes.

3. Garnish each bowl with fresh chives.

DID YOU KNOW?

You can make use of all parts of fennel: the bottom portion is typically sliced or chopped and used in soups and salads; the stalks can be used to make vegetable broth and then removed; and then finally the fronds can be used as an herb like dill.

PER SERVING (⅛ OF RECIPE):

56 calories	1.5 g protein	822 mg sodium
0.2 g fat	13.2 g carbohydrate	40 mg calcium
0 g saturated fat	5.8 g sugar	0.6 mg iron
3.2% calories from fat	2.5 g fiber	18.7 mg vitamin C
0 mg cholesterol		3892 mcg beta-carotene
		0.7 mg vitamin E

TOASTY TORTILLA SOUP

MAKES FOUR 1-CUP SERVINGS ■ **PREPARATION TIME: 20 minutes** ■ **COOK TIME: 50 minutes**

You'll tip your sombrero to the toasty and tasty tortilla strips topping this colorful and flavorful soup. Although beans are not traditional in tortilla soup, they increase the fiber significantly.

4½ cups vegetable broth

1 small onion, chopped

2 garlic cloves, minced

2 teaspoons chili powder

1 (15-ounce) can diced tomatoes

1 medium zucchini, chopped

1 medium yellow squash, chopped

1 cup frozen corn, thawed

1 (15-ounce) can red kidney beans, drained and rinsed

Kosher salt to taste

Freshly ground black pepper to taste

2 corn tortillas

1. Heat ½ cup broth in a large saucepan over medium heat. Add onion and sauté for 3 minutes. Add garlic and chili powder and cook for 2 minutes.
2. Add all remaining ingredients except tortillas and bring to a boil. Lower heat and simmer for 25 minutes.
3. Meanwhile, preheat the oven to 350°F. Cut each tortilla into ½-inch strips. Place strips on a baking sheet and bake for 5 to 6 minutes, until brown.
4. To serve: ladle soup into bowls and top with a few tortilla strips.

DID YOU KNOW?

Keep your chili powder stored in the refrigerator to preserve its color as well as its flavor. In fact, other red-colored spices, such as paprika, also fare well stored in the refrigerator.

PER SERVING (¼ OF RECIPE):

218 calories	10.3 g protein	1464 mg sodium
1.6 g fat	45.2 g carbohydrate	114 mg calcium
0.3 g saturated fat	10.7 g sugar	3.7 mg iron
6.3% calories from fat	9.8 g fiber	21.1 mg vitamin C
0 mg cholesterol		944 mcg beta-carotene
		1.4 mg vitamin E

DINNER

7

WHEN I (NEAL) WAS a child, growing up in North Dakota, dinners were not very adventurous: meat, potatoes, and corn. Or meat, potatoes, and green beans. Or meat, potatoes, and more meat and potatoes.

Today, we expect more. We can draw inspiration from novel ingredients and products from all around the globe. Let us encourage you to experiment with new flavors and new preparation techniques. These recipes will allow you to discover many treasures.

As you plan your meals, you can really follow your tastes. All the recipes here are healthful. But, for balance, let me encourage you to think about four food groups—grains, legumes (beans, peas, or lentils), vegetables, and fruits. It is good to include them all at each meal. Or perhaps have grains, beans, and vegetables in the main meal, with fruit as a dessert or snack.

So dinner might be a pasta (grain) dish, such as Fettuccine with Roasted Peppers and Zucchini (page 105) or Italian Fusilli with Sun-Dried Tomatoes and Artichoke Hearts (page 106). Serve it along with, say, chickpeas (a bean dish), and one or two vegetables. Dessert might be Fruit Kabobs with Peach Cream Dip (page 167) or Chocolate Cherry Nirvana (page 168).

Another menu might include a rice dish, along with Sweet and Sour Tofu (page 152) which counts as a legume, since it is from soybeans, with sides of broccoli or spinach (or both), and a simple fruit dessert or something more elaborate, such as our Baked Apples in Phyllo Dough (page 172).

There is no need to stick to rigid serving sizes. Just include these four food groups, and your body will take care of the rest.

Technology can be a time-saver: If you have a rice cooker with a built-in timer and a slow-cooker, just set them up in the morning, and your dinner will be ready when you get home. When you find a new favorite recipe, you may wish to prepare extra to save for later in conveniently sized containers. Freezing and reheating is a snap, so every night can mean a healthful feast, even if you barely lift a finger.

Delicious soups, pizzas, sides, and main dishes—they are all here, waiting for you to enjoy.

FETTUCCINE WITH ROASTED PEPPERS AND ZUCCHINI

MAKES 4 SERVINGS ■ **PREPARATION TIME: 15 minutes** ■ **COOK TIME: 50 minutes**

This sauce in this pasta dish really puts canned spaghetti sauce to shame. The flavors from the roasted peppers will lure you in and keep you coming back to this recipe over and over! The fresh thyme really puts it over the top.

1 large red bell pepper

1 large yellow bell pepper

¼ cup vegetable broth

1 large onion, halved and sliced

3 garlic cloves, minced

2 medium zucchini, sliced into ¼-inch-thick rounds

Pinch crushed red pepper

½ cup dry white wine

1 tablespoon lemon juice

2 teaspoons fresh thyme

1 (10-ounce) package fettuccine pasta, preferably whole wheat

Kosher or sea salt to taste

Freshly ground black pepper to taste

DID YOU KNOW?

Fettuccine means "little ribbons" in Italian. And yes, you really can have pasta: its low glycemic index means it releases natural sugars nice and slowly.

1. To prepare the bell peppers, there are two options: Place whole peppers directly on the burner of a gas stovetop or on a gas or charcoal grill. With long-handled tongs, keep turning the peppers until they are blackened. Put the roasted peppers into a bowl, cover with plastic wrap, and allow the peppers to cool.

   ALTERNATIVE METHOD: Cut the peppers in half and remove the seeds and white membrane. Place the pepper halves on a broiler pan. Broil the peppers skin-side up until the skin blackens. Place the pepper halves in a bowl, cover with plastic wrap, and allow to cool.

2. When the peppers have cooled enough to handle, remove the blackened skin with your fingertips and cut each pepper into four pieces. Discard the seeds and white membrane if you haven't done so already. Cut the peppers into 1 inch strips and set aside.

3. Heat the vegetable broth in a large skillet over medium heat. Put in the onion and garlic and sauté for 5 to 6 minutes. Add the zucchini and crushed red pepper and sauté for about 15 minutes. Add the roasted peppers, wine, lemon juice, and thyme. Sauté for 1 minute.

4. Cook the fettuccine according to package directions. Drain the pasta, immediately toss with the vegetable mixture, and serve.

PER SERVING (¼ OF RECIPE):

397 calories	13.6 g protein	216 mg sodium
2.2 g fat	76 g carbohydrate	50 mg calcium
0.4 g saturated fat	9.6 g sugar	3.6 mg iron
4.6% calories from fat	6.3 g fiber	143.4 mg vitamin C
0 mg cholesterol		1248 mcg beta-carotene
		1 mg vitamin E

ITALIAN FUSILLI WITH SUN-DRIED TOMATOES AND ARTICHOKE HEARTS

MAKES FOUR 2-CUP SERVINGS ■ PREPARATION TIME: 20 minutes ■ COOK TIME: 15 minutes

The sun-dried tomatoes and artichokes in this dish make the perfect couple. The flavors are even more striking the next day.

½ cup sun-dried tomatoes

¼ cup vegetable broth

1 medium onion, coarsely chopped

3 garlic cloves, minced

1 (14-ounce) can artichoke hearts, drained and quartered

½ cup dry white wine

Sea salt to taste

Freshly ground black pepper to taste

2 teaspoons chopped fresh oregano

¼ cup loosely packed fresh basil, thinly sliced

1 (10-ounce) package fusilli pasta, preferably whole wheat

1. Cover the sun-dried tomatoes with boiling water in a small bowl and let stand for about 10 minutes to soften. Drain and slice tomatoes into thin strips. Set aside.

2. Heat the broth over medium-high heat. Add the onion and garlic and sauté for 3 to 5 minutes, until softened and translucent. Add the tomatoes, artichoke hearts, wine, salt, and black pepper. Lower heat and simmer for 5 minutes. Stir in the oregano and basil.

3. Meanwhile cook the pasta according to package directions until al dente. Drain. Toss the pasta with the artichoke mixture.

DID YOU KNOW?

Sun-dried tomatoes were born in Italy as a way to store fresh tomatoes for the winter.

PER SERVING (¼ OF RECIPE):		
401 calories	14.8 g protein	525 mg sodium
2.3 g fat	76.3 g carbohydrate	54 mg calcium
0.4 g saturated fat	5.7 g sugar	3.9 mg iron
4.9% calories from fat	10.6 g fiber	10 mg vitamin C
0 mg cholesterol		111 mcg beta-carotene
		0.3 mg vitamin E

TOMATOES STUFFED WITH FRENCH LENTILS

MAKES 4 SERVINGS ■ **PREPARATION TIME: 15 minutes** ■ **COOK TIME: 35 minutes plus cooling**

What's better than an edible container? These hollowed tomatoes are a perfect vessel for a refreshing lentil salad. Bell pepper and celery add a nice crunch to the creamy lentils.

4 large tomatoes

1 cup dried French lentils (sometimes known as du Puy lentils)

2 bay leaves

1 tablespoon chopped onion

1 tablespoon balsamic vinegar

2 tablespoons fresh lemon juice

1 tablespoon stone-ground mustard

1 garlic clove, finely minced

Pinch of crushed red pepper

Kosher or sea salt to taste

Freshly ground black pepper to taste

1 small red bell pepper, chopped

1 celery stalk, finely chopped

1. To prepare the tomatoes: With a paring knife, cut the tops off the tomatoes. With a melon baller, scoop out the insides of the tomatoes, leaving a shell thick enough to hold lentils. Place tomatoes upside down onto paper towels to drain for 30 minutes.

2. Meanwhile, sort and rinse the lentils. Bring 2 cups water to a boil. Add the lentils, bay leaves, and onion and bring to another boil. Lower heat, cover, and simmer for about 20 minutes. The lentils should be cooked through, but still firm. Drain the lentils and shake gently to remove the excess water. Remove bay leaves.

3. In a small bowl, whisk the vinegar, lemon juice, mustard, garlic, crushed red pepper, salt, and black pepper. Pour over the lentils. Stir and cool.

4. Add the bell pepper and celery to cooled lentil mixture.

5. Divide the lentil mixture evenly among tomatoes and serve.

DID YOU KNOW?

When choosing tomatoes for this recipe, look for firm tomatoes. They are sturdier and won't break apart. French lentils are smaller in size and are firmer, therefore less likely to break down in a salad. Like other lentils, they are rich in protein.

PER SERVING (¼ OF RECIPE):

200 calories	14.1 g protein	224 mg sodium
1 g fat	36.6 g carbohydrate	55 mg calcium
0.1 g saturated fat	6.5 g sugar	5.8 mg iron
4% calories from fat	9.7 g fiber	65.6 mg vitamin C
0 mg cholesterol		823 mcg beta-carotene
		1.3 mg vitamin E

CAJUN CORN AND EDAMAME SAUTÉ

MAKES 4 SERVINGS ■ **PREPARATION TIME: 15 minutes** ■ **COOK TIME: 30 minutes**

You may think of edamame as a delicacy served only in Japanese restaurants, but you can easily make this dish at home as a meal or a side dish.

Olive oil cooking spray

1 small onion, chopped

1 celery stalk, chopped

1 small green bell pepper, chopped

1 garlic clove, minced

⅔ cup frozen shelled edamame, thawed

3 medium ears of corn, kernels cut off the cob

½ teaspoon Cajun seasoning

½ cup vegetable broth

1 tomato, chopped

1 tablespoon finely chopped fresh parsley

Kosher or sea salt to taste

Freshly ground black pepper to taste

1. Coat a large skillet with cooking spray, and heat it over medium-high heat. Sauté the onion, celery, bell pepper, and garlic for 5 minutes. Add the edamame, Cajun seasoning, and corn and cook for 8 minutes.

2. Pour in the vegetable broth. Reduce the heat to low and simmer for 5 minutes. Add the tomato and simmer for 5 more minutes, until the vegetable broth is mostly absorbed and vegetables are tender. Add the parsley. Season with salt and black pepper.

DID YOU KNOW?

Studies show that girls who consume soy products during adolescence have about 30% less risk of breast cancer in adulthood.

PER SERVING (¼ OF RECIPE):

137 calories	6.2 g protein	350 mg sodium
2.5 g fat	27 g carbohydrate	35 mg calcium
0.3 g saturated fat	5.6 g sugar	1.4 mg iron
15.1% calories from fat	5.5 g fiber	28.9 mg vitamin C
0 mg cholesterol		335 mcg beta-carotene
		0.6 mg vitamin E

QUINOA WITH NAVY BEANS AND ALMONDS

MAKES 4 SERVINGS ■ PREPARATION TIME: 15 minutes ■ COOK TIME: 25 minutes

This quinoa dish is quick to prepare and good for both your budget and your figure.

1 cup quinoa, rinsed in a fine sieve

¼ cup vegetable broth

1 cup sliced cremini mushrooms

½ cup chopped onion

½ cup chopped red bell pepper

2 tablespoons lemon juice

1 (15-ounce) can white navy beans, drained and rinsed

Kosher or sea salt to taste

Freshly ground black pepper to taste

1 tablespoon toasted slivered almonds

2 tablespoons finely chopped fresh parsley

1. Bring 2 cups of water to a boil in a small saucepan. Add the rinsed quinoa, bring to a boil again, lower the heat, cover, and simmer for 15 minutes.

2. Meanwhile, heat the vegetable broth in a medium skillet over medium heat. Add the mushrooms and sauté for 2 minutes. Add the onion and bell pepper and sauté for 5 minutes until the mushrooms are browned. Add the lemon juice, beans, and cooked quinoa. Season with salt and black pepper and mix well. Garnish with the almonds and parsley and serve.

DID YOU KNOW?

Quinoa is part of the goosefoot species. It is grown mostly for its seeds, but the leaves of the plant can also be eaten. If someone in your family follows a gluten-free diet, quinoa is a perfect choice.

PER SERVING (¼ OF RECIPE):

286 calories	13.1 g protein	355 mg sodium
4 g fat	50.9 g carbohydrate	88 mg calcium
0.5 g saturated fat	5.3 g sugar	4.2 mg iron
12.3% calories from fat	11.6 g fiber	37.1 mg vitamin C
0 mg cholesterol		387 mcg beta-carotene
		1.8 mg vitamin E

SOBA NOODLES WITH CHINESE VEGETABLES

MAKES FOUR 2-CUP SERVINGS ■ PREPARATION TIME: 15 minutes ■ COOK TIME: 15 minutes

This Asian-inspired dish is loaded with colorful vegetables that are left al dente for a great texture. It can be enjoyed hot or chilled.

1 (8-ounce) package soba noodles

½ cup vegetable broth

1 small leek, white part only, washed and thinly sliced

1 tablespoon fresh peeled minced ginger

2 garlic cloves, minced

2 medium carrots, peeled, cut on a diagonal into half-moon slices

1 red bell pepper, cut into strips

1 cup sugar snap peas

1 cup sliced savoy cabbage

2 tablespoons reduced-sodium soy sauce

2 teaspoons light brown sugar

Cilantro leaves for garnish

1. Cook the noodles according to package directions. Drain, rinse, and set aside.
2. Heat ¼ cup broth in a wok or heavy skillet over medium-high heat. Add the leek and stir-fry for 2 minutes. Add the ginger, garlic, and carrots and stir-fry for 2 minutes.
3. Put in the bell pepper, snap peas, cabbage, and remaining ¼ cup broth. Cover and steam vegetables until they are tender, about 3 to 5 minutes. Add soy sauce and sugar and cook for 1 minute. Add the noodles to reheat.
4. Transfer the noodles onto a platter and top with cilantro to serve.

DID YOU KNOW?

Soba noodles are a staple in Japanese cuisine. Unlike traditional wheat noodles, soba noodles are made primarily from buckwheat flour—resulting in a lower gluten content. The noodles are thin and resemble whole wheat spaghetti in color and shape.

PER SERVING (¼ OF RECIPE):

229 calories	9.8 g protein	411 mg sodium
1 g fat	49.4 g carbohydrate	53 mg calcium
0.2 g saturated fat	6.9 g sugar	2.5 mg iron
3.7% calories from fat	6.4 g fiber	60.9 mg vitamin C
0 mg cholesterol		2953 mcg beta-carotene
		1.3 mg vitamin E

UDON NOODLES WITH SHIITAKE AND BUTTON MUSHROOMS

MAKES FOUR 1½-CUP SERVINGS ■ **PREPARATION TIME: 15 minutes** ■ **COOK TIME: 25 minutes**

This dish combines the earthy flavor of mushrooms with the sweetness of mirin and the heat of ginger. Serve it hot or cold.

1 (8-ounce) package udon noodles

1¼ cups vegetable broth

1 tablespoon minced garlic

1 small onion, halved and thinly sliced

1 tablespoon black bean sauce

2 teaspoons minced fresh ginger

1 small carrot, peeled and sliced into ¼-inch slices

1 cup thinly sliced shiitake mushroom caps

1 cup thinly sliced button mushroom caps

¼ cup mirin

1 tablespoon soy sauce

2 scallions, thinly sliced

2 teaspoons chopped toasted almonds

1. Cook udon noodles according to package directions. Drain and set aside.
2. Heat ¼ cup broth in a large skillet over medium heat. Put in the garlic, onion, and black bean sauce and cook for 2 minutes. Add the ginger and cook for 2 minutes.
3. Add the carrot and cook for 3 minutes. Add the mushrooms and cook for 3 minutes. Stir in the mirin and cook until it evaporates.
4. Add the remaining 1 cup broth and the soy sauce and cook for 2 minutes. Gently add noodles and toss to combine.
5. Serve noodles topped with scallions and almonds.

DID YOU KNOW?

Shiitake mushrooms are considered a symbol of longevity in Asia. They have a rich and smoky flavor, and are a good source of selenium, a cancer-fighting mineral.

PER SERVING (¼ OF RECIPE):

240 calories	9.6 g protein	569 mg sodium
1.8 g fat	47.8 g carbohydrate	48 mg calcium
0.3 g saturated fat	3.7 g sugar	2.3 mg iron
6.4% calories from fat	5.7 g fiber	4.1 mg vitamin C
0 mg cholesterol		1084 mcg beta-carotene
		1 mg vitamin E

SWEET POTATOES AND CHICKPEAS IN CHILI SAUCE

MAKES 10 SERVINGS ■ PREPARATION TIME: 20 minutes ■ COOK TIME: 40 minutes

This is a great meal when you are craving a flavorful and filling comfort food.

¾ cup vegetable broth

½ cup chopped celery

½ teaspoon crushed fennel seeds

3 garlic cloves, minced

¾ cup chopped red onions

½ teaspoon ground turmeric

¼ teaspoon paprika

1 chipotle pepper in adobo sauce, chopped

2 pounds sweet potatoes, peeled and cut into 1-inch cubes

1 (15-ounce) can chickpeas, drained

¼ cup chopped fresh parsley

Kosher or sea salt to taste

Freshly ground black pepper to taste

1. Heat ¼ cup of the broth in a Dutch oven over medium heat. Add the celery, fennel seeds, and garlic and cook for 2 minutes. Add the onions, turmeric, paprika, and chipotle pepper. Cook for 5 minutes, stirring occasionally.

2. Add the sweet potatoes and the remaining ½ cup broth, cover, reduce the heat, and simmer for about 25 minutes, stirring occasionally until sweet potatoes are tender. Add the chickpeas and continue to cook for 5 minutes. Add the parsley and season with salt and black pepper.

DID YOU KNOW?

A chipotle pepper is a jalapeño that has been dried and smoked. It is easy to find them pickled and canned in adobo sauce. Add more or less depending on your taste.

PER SERVING (¹⁄₁₀ OF RECIPE):

112 calories	3.9 g protein	301 mg sodium
0.9 g fat	22.8 g carbohydrate	46 mg calcium
0.1 g saturated fat	5.2 g sugar	1.7 mg iron
7.1% calories from fat	4.1 g fiber	14.2 mg vitamin C
0 mg cholesterol		6818 mcg beta-carotene
		0.9 mg vitamin E

ASIAN BROTH WITH MUSHROOMS, TOFU, AND GINGER

MAKES FOUR 1-CUP SERVINGS ■ **PREPARATION TIME: 20 minutes** ■ **COOK TIME: 15 minutes**

This soup has a wonderfully authentic flavor. And it accommodates leftover veggies very well. Button mushrooms and portobello mushrooms would also do well in this soup.

4 cups vegetable broth

1 cup sliced shiitake mushroom caps

1 cup coarsely chopped oyster mushrooms

1 cup sliced cremini mushrooms

1 shallot, finely chopped

1 cup thinly sliced carrots

½ (8-ounce) package udon noodles

2 tablespoons minced fresh ginger

2 teaspoons red curry paste, or 1 small hot pepper of your choice, finely chopped

2 tablespoons reduced-sodium soy sauce

2 tablespoons rice vinegar

4 ounces extra-firm tofu, cut into ½-inch cubes

1. Heat ½ cup broth in a large saucepan over medium heat. Add the mushrooms and shallot and sauté for 5 to 6 minutes, until mushrooms are browned.

2. Add 3 cups water and the remaining 3½ cups broth to the mushroom mixture and bring to a boil. Add the carrots, noodles, ginger, and red curry paste. Reduce heat and simmer for 7 to 8 minutes. Drizzle the soup with soy sauce and vinegar. Add tofu and heat for 2 to 3 minutes.

DID YOU KNOW?

Studies show that ½ teaspoon (0.5 g) of ginger taken daily helps prevent seasickness. Start a few days before you embark.

PER SERVING (¼ OF RECIPE):

171 calories	8.9 g protein	1278 mg sodium
2.3 g fat	31.3 g carbohydrate	90 mg calcium
0.3 g saturated fat	5.7 g sugar	2.1 mg iron
11.2% calories from fat	4.3 g fiber	3.3 mg vitamin C
0 mg cholesterol		2623 mcg beta-carotene
		0.6 mg vitamin E

CARAMELIZED ONIONS WITH LENTILS AND BROWN RICE

MAKES SIX 1-CUP SERVINGS ■ PREPARATION TIME: 15 minutes ■ COOK TIME: 1 hour

This is a wholesome, simple, hearty dish that will warm you in cold winter months. This recipe caramelizes onions without oil!

1 cup vegetable broth

7 cups sliced onions (about 4 large onions)

1 cup long-grain brown rice

1½ cups dried red or yellow lentils

Kosher salt to taste

Freshly ground black pepper to taste

1. Heat ½ cup broth in a large skillet over medium-low heat. Add the onions, cover, and cook for 20 minutes until soft, stirring occasionally and adding more broth if necessary. Uncover and increase heat to medium and cook for 30 minutes, until very brown, stirring occasionally, adding more broth as needed.

2. While the onions are cooking, bring 4½ cups water to a boil in a large saucepan. Add the rice, cover, and cook for 25 minutes. Stir in the lentils, cover, and cook for an additional 20 to 25 minutes. Stir in ½ cup of the cooked onions and cook for an additional 5 minutes. Season with salt and black pepper. Spoon the rice and lentil dish onto a platter and top with the remaining cooked onions.

DID YOU KNOW?

The word *lentil* comes from Latin, referring to its lenslike shape.

PER SERVING (⅙ OF RECIPE):

340 calories	16.8 g protein	324 mg sodium
1.7 g fat	67.1 g carbohydrate	77 mg calcium
0.3 g saturated fat	8.9 g sugar	5.3 mg iron
4.3% calories from fat	13.5 g fiber	10.3 mg vitamin C
0 mg cholesterol		49 mcg beta-carotene
		0.2 mg vitamin E

CASSOULET

MAKES SIX 1-CUP SERVINGS ■ **PREPARATION TIME: 10 minutes** ■ **COOK TIME: 45 minutes**

This hearty stew will fill your home with the most wonderful scent. Served in a Dutch oven, you can feed large groups easily.

1¼ cups vegetable broth

1 large onion, chopped

2 carrots, sliced diagonally into ½-inch-thick slices

3 garlic cloves, minced

3 cups cooked great northern beans or 2 (15.5-ounce) cans (if canned, drain and rinse)

¾ teaspoon dried thyme

Kosher salt to taste

Freshly ground black pepper to taste

1 (28-ounce) can diced tomatoes, with liquid

1 bay leaf

2 vegetarian sausage links, sliced

2 tablespoons finely chopped fresh parsley

¼ cup whole wheat bread crumbs, toasted

1. Heat ¼ cup broth in a large Dutch oven over medium heat. Add the onion, carrots, and garlic and sauté for 5 minutes.
2. Add the remaining 1 cup broth, beans, thyme, salt, black pepper, tomatoes, and bay leaf. Bring to a boil, lower heat, and simmer, covered, for 45 minutes.
3. Remove the bay leaf and add the vegetarian sausage. Cook for 2 minutes. Garnish each serving with parsley and bread crumbs.

DID YOU KNOW?

Cassoulet is a rich, slow-cooked stew or casserole originating in the south of France

PER SERVING (⅙ OF RECIPE):

212 calories	15.8 g protein	788 mg sodium
2.3 g fat	34.7 g carbohydrate	156 mg calcium
0.4 g saturated fat	6.2 g sugar	5.6 mg iron
9.6% calories from fat	8.2 g fiber	16.3 mg vitamin C
0 mg cholesterol		1765 mcg beta-carotene
		2.2 mg vitamin E

CURRIED TEMPEH KABOBS

MAKES 4 SERVINGS ■ **PREPARATION TIME: 20 minutes** ■ **COOK TIME: 20 minutes**

Toss these kabobs on the grill for a tasty summer meal. Add whatever vegetables you have on hand to fill out the kabobs. Serve with brown rice, couscous, or pita bread.

FOR THE MARINADE:

1 teaspoon coconut extract mixed with ¾ cup soy milk, or ¾ cup canned lite coconut milk

1 (8-ounce) can tomato sauce

1 garlic clove, minced, or 1 teaspoon garlic powder

1 to 3 tablespoons curry powder or garam masala powder

1 teaspoon ground black pepper

1 teaspoon ground cumin (optional)

1 teaspoon onion powder (optional)

FOR THE KABOBS:

1 (8-ounce) package tempeh, cut into 1 x 2-inch cubes

1 onion, cut into wedges

12 cherry or grape tomatoes

12 mushrooms

1 bell pepper, seeded and cut into wedges

1. In a small bowl, mix together all marinade ingredients.
2. Begin to assemble kabobs by placing vegetables and tempeh on skewers.
3. Soak kabobs in marinade for a minimum of 15 minutes, or up to one day in the refrigerator.
4. When ready to cook kabobs, preheat the broiler or grill to medium high.
5. Cook for 10 minutes, turning and brushing with marinade as needed. Cook for 10 additional minutes and remove from heat. Serve immediately.

DID YOU KNOW?

If using wooden skewers, soak them in water to prevent burning. Also, blanching the tempeh before marinating it will cut down on bitterness. To do this, bring 1 quart of water to boil. Add tempeh, turn off heat, let stand for 1 minute, then drain.

PER SERVING (¼ OF RECIPE):

186 calories	14.4 g protein	327 mg sodium
7.3 g fat	20 g carbohydrate	134 mg calcium
1.4 g saturated fat	7.3 g sugar	4.1 mg iron
32.7% calories from fat	5.5 g fiber	37.6 mg vitamin C
0 mg cholesterol		321 mcg beta-carotene
		2.1 mg vitamin E

ROBYN'S FIRST TRIP to Italy was a wonderful adventure involving lots of delicious foods, but what she remembers most are the amazing pizzas. Not only are they mostly cheeseless, but they are loaded with tons of veggies, garlic, and herbs.

Allow us to give you a few pointers as you begin the journey to your own slice of Italy. When making your dough, keep it in a draft-free place while it rises and don't allow it to rise any more than double the size or it will become too "yeasty." You can freeze the dough for up to two months. Feel free to use all whole wheat flour if you like, but experiment with the recipe as written the first time so you have a good feel for it. Use your imagination; any veggies can go on a pizza!

PIZZA TIME

PIZZA DOUGH

2 teaspoons agave nectar

1 (¼-ounce) package active dry yeast

1 cup whole wheat flour

1 cup unbleached all-purpose flour (preferably organic)

1 teaspoon salt

Vegetable oil cooking spray

2 tablespoons yellow cornmeal

1. In a large bowl, dissolve the agave nectar and yeast in ¾ cup warm water (100°–110°F). Let stand for 5 minutes. Add the flours and salt to the yeast mixture and stir until a soft dough forms. Turn dough out onto a lightly floured surface. Knead until smooth and elastic, adding more flour if necessary to prevent sticking. Dough will feel slightly sticky.

2. Place dough in a large bowl coated with cooking spray, turning to coat the top. Cover with a towel and let rise in a draft-free place until double in size, about 30 to 40 minutes.

3. Punch down the dough and roll into a 10- or 11-inch circle on a lightly floured surface. Place dough on a baking sheet covered with parchment paper and sprinkled with cornmeal. Crimp edges to form a rim. Lightly spray the surface of the dough with cooking spray. Continue with the following recipe of your choice.

KALAMATA OLIVE, CAPER, AND BASIL PIZZA

MAKES ONE 10- OR 11-INCH PIZZA ■ PREPARATION TIME: 10 minutes ■ COOK TIME: 5 minutes

1 recipe Pizza Dough
(page 118)

½ cup tomato sauce

1 cup halved Kalamata
olives

1 tablespoon capers

7 large basil leaves, torn

1. Preheat the oven to 500°F.
2. Cover pizza dough with tomato sauce, then scatter on the olives and capers. Bake for 4 minutes.
3. Place the basil on the pizza and bake for another minute.

PER SERVING (⅙ OF PIZZA):

197 calories	6.1 g protein	743 mg sodium
3.1 g fat	37.8 g carbohydrate	41 mg calcium
0.4 g saturated fat	2.4 g sugar	3.2 mg iron
13.4% calories from fat	4.5 g fiber	1.8 mg vitamin C
0 mg cholesterol		120 mcg beta-carotene
		0.9 mg vitamin E

EGGPLANT, ARTICHOKE, RED PEPPER, AND BLACK OLIVE PIZZA

MAKES ONE 10- OR 11-INCH PIZZA ■ PREPARATION TIME: 20 minutes ■ COOK TIME: 20 minutes

2 cups chopped eggplant

1 cup tomato sauce

Pinch of crushed red pepper

Pinch of sugar

1 recipe Pizza Dough (page 118)

1 cup tightly packed, roughly chopped spinach

½ red bell pepper, seeded and thinly sliced

½ cup quartered artichoke hearts

¼ cup thinly sliced red onion

¼ cup pitted and quartered black olives

1. In a medium nonstick skillet, bring 2 tablespoons water to a simmer. Add the eggplant and cook until water evaporates, approximately 3 minutes. Add the tomato sauce, crushed red pepper, and sugar. Continue to cook until eggplant is soft, about 7 minutes. Cool.

2. Preheat oven to 500°F.

3. Cover pizza dough with eggplant sauce, then top with spinach, bell pepper, artichoke hearts, onion, and black olives. Bake for 10 to 12 minutes, or until crust is golden brown.

PER SERVING (⅙ OF PIZZA):

206 calories	7.1 g protein	701 mg sodium
1.5 g fat	43.2 g carbohydrate	39 mg calcium
0.2 g saturated fat	5.4 g sugar	3.1 mg iron
6.2% calories from fat	6.4 g fiber	22.2 mg vitamin C
0 mg cholesterol		540 mcg beta-carotene
		1.2 mg vitamin E

CARAMELIZED ONION, ARUGULA, AND CHERRY TOMATO PIZZA

MAKES ONE 10- OR 11-INCH PIZZA ■ PREPARATION TIME: 20 minutes ■ COOK TIME: 20 to 25 minutes

1 large sweet onion, thinly sliced

¼ cup plus 1 tablespoon balsamic vinegar

Black pepper to taste

1 recipe Pizza Dough (page 118)

1 cup tightly packed baby arugula

1 cup halved cherry tomatoes

¼ cup pitted and quartered black olives

1 tablespoon pine nuts, slightly toasted

1. In a large skillet, bring ¼ cup water to a simmer over medium heat. Add the onion and cook until water evaporates, approximately 3 to 4 minutes. Add ¼ cup balsamic vinegar, sugar, and black pepper. Continue to cook, stirring often until onion is soft and caramelized, about 8 minutes. Cool.

2. Preheat the oven to 500°F.

3. Bake the pizza dough for 8 minutes. Remove from the oven, spread with caramelized onions, and top with arugula, tomatoes, olives, and pine nuts. Bake for an additional 4 to 5 minutes. Drizzle with remaining 1 tablespoon balsamic vinegar before serving.

PER SERVING (⅙ OF PIZZA):

209 calories	6.5 g protein	454 mg sodium
2.3 g fat	41.4 g carbohydrate	39 mg calcium
0.3 g saturated fat	5.3 g sugar	2.9 mg iron
9.4% calories from fat	4.2 g fiber	7.1 mg vitamin C
0 mg cholesterol		135 mcg beta-carotene
		0.5 mg vitamin E

YELLOW PEPPER, MUSHROOM, TOMATO, SPINACH, AND BASIL PIZZA

MAKES ONE 10- OR 11-INCH PIZZA ■ PREPARATION TIME: 15 minutes ■ COOK TIME: 10 minutes

1 recipe Pizza Dough (page 118)

1 cup canned tomato sauce

2 garlic cloves, thinly sliced

½ yellow bell pepper, thinly sliced

½ small onion, thinly sliced

1 cup thinly sliced mushrooms

½ cup halved cherry tomatoes

1 cup roughly chopped spinach

1 teaspoon dried oregano

10 fresh basil leaves, torn

1. Preheat the oven to 500°F.
2. Cover pizza dough with tomato sauce, then top with garlic, bell pepper, onion, mushrooms, tomatoes, and spinach. Sprinkle with oregano. Bake for 8 minutes.
3. Take pizza out of the oven, top with basil, and bake for another 1 to 2 minutes.

PER SERVING (⅙ OF RECIPE):		
187 calories	6.8 g protein	616 mg sodium
0.9 g fat	39.8 g carbohydrate	34 mg calcium
0.1 g saturated fat	4.4 g sugar	3.1 mg iron
4% calories from fat	4.7 g fiber	21.6 mg vitamin C
0 mg cholesterol		433 mcg beta-carotene
		1 mg vitamin E

PEPPER, MUSHROOM, TOMATO, SPINACH, AND GARLIC PIZZA

MAKES ONE 10- OR 11-INCH PIZZA ■ PREPARATION TIME: 15 minutes ■ COOK TIME: 8 to 10 minutes

1 recipe Pizza Dough (page 118)

1 cup canned tomato sauce

½ yellow pepper, thinly sliced

½ red pepper, thinly sliced

1 cup thinly sliced mushrooms

½ cup halved cherry tomatoes

1 cup roughly chopped spinach

2 garlic cloves, thinly sliced

1. Preheat the oven to 500°F.
2. Cover the pizza dough with tomato sauce, then top with bell peppers, mushrooms, tomatoes, spinach, and garlic. Bake for 8 minutes.

PER SERVING (⅙ OF PIZZA):		
187 calories	6.8 g protein	616 mg sodium
0.9 g fat	39.8 g carbohydrate	30 mg calcium
0.1 g saturated fat	4.8 g sugar	3 mg iron
3.9% calories from fat	4.6 g fiber	37.4 mg vitamin C
0 mg cholesterol		545 mcg beta-carotene
		1.1 mg vitamin E

GRILLED TOFU WITH SMOKY BARBECUE SAUCE

MAKES 4 SERVINGS ■ PREPARATION TIME: 5 minutes ■ COOK TIME: 10 minutes

The tofu in this dish is best grilled, but can also be baked. Making your own barbeque sauce is easy and economical.

FOR THE BARBECUE SAUCE:

1 (8-ounce) can tomato paste

½ cup agave nectar

1 teaspoon liquid smoke

½ teaspoon ground cinnamon

½ teaspoon ground allspice

2 garlic cloves, minced

2 tablespoons tamari

Pinch of cayenne pepper

FOR THE KABOBS:

1 pound extra-firm tofu, pressed

Wooden skewers, soaked for 1 hour in warm water

Vegetable oil cooking spray

1. Combine all the barbecue sauce ingredients in a small saucepan. Bring to a boil over medium heat. Lower heat to simmer and cook for 5 minutes, stirring regularly. Set aside.
2. Cut the tofu into equal-size slabs, about ¾-inch thick. Using two wooden skewers per tofu piece, skewer tofu, separating skewers about ½ inch from each other.
3. Coat a grill rack with cooking spray. Preheat gas grill to medium-high heat. When the grill is ready, add the tofu and grill for 1 minute. Brush some of the barbecue sauce on the top and cook for 1 more minute. Turn the tofu and brush with more barbecue sauce. Cook for 2 additional minutes, until the tofu is browned.

DID YOU KNOW?

Liquid smoke adds a natural smoky flavor to the barbecue sauce.

PER SERVING (¼ OF RECIPE):

280 calories	14.3 g protein	922 mg sodium
7 g fat	46 g carbohydrate	314 mg calcium
0.7 g saturated fat	30.1 g sugar	6 mg iron
20.8% calories from fat	3.1 g fiber	13.6 mg vitamin C
0 mg cholesterol		524 mcg beta-carotene
		2.5 mg vitamin E

ITALIAN BEANS AND GREENS

MAKES 4 SERVINGS ■ **PREPARATION TIME: 10 minutes** ■ **COOK TIME: 15 minutes**

The rich, peppery taste of arugula pairs nicely with the chickpeas and tomatoes in this colorful dish.

¼ cup vegetable broth

1 small onion, chopped

2 garlic cloves, minced

6 cups baby arugula, washed

2 (15-ounce) cans chickpeas, drained and rinsed

1 (10-ounce) can diced tomatoes, drained, or 2 medium tomatoes, chopped

½ teaspoon dried oregano

½ teaspoon dried basil

Pinch of sugar

Kosher or sea salt to taste

Freshly ground black pepper to taste

1. Heat the broth in a large skillet over medium heat. Add the onion and garlic and sauté for 3 minutes. Add the arugula and lower heat to medium-low. Cook until the arugula is almost wilted.

2. Add the chickpeas, tomatoes, oregano, basil, sugar, salt, and black pepper. Cover and cook for 5 minutes until all ingredients are heated through.

DID YOU KNOW?

Unripe (or green) chickpeas are called *guasana* in Mexico and other Latin American countries, and are often eaten raw—right out of the pod.

PER SERVING (¼ OF RECIPE):

264 calories	14.3 g protein	391 mg sodium
4.1 g fat	45.2 g carbohydrate	145 mg calcium
0.4 g saturated fat	3.3 g sugar	5.3 mg iron
12.9% calories from fat	10.3 g fiber	12.3 mg vitamin C
0 mg cholesterol		510 mcg beta-carotene
		1 mg vitamin E

MIXED VEGETABLE CURRY
WITH WHOLE WHEAT COUSCOUS

MAKES 6 SERVINGS ■ PREPARATION TIME: 15 minutes ■ COOK TIME: 30 minutes

This one-pot dish is tasty hot or cold, and boasts a rainbow of colors.

1 cup vegetable broth

1 cup chopped onion

2 garlic cloves, minced

1 tablespoon ground coriander

1 teaspoon cumin seeds

½ teaspoon ground turmeric

Sea salt to taste

Freshly ground black pepper to taste

2 medium tomatoes, seeded and cut into 1-inch pieces

2 cups frozen green peas

1 medium sweet potato, peeled and cut into 1-inch cubes

1 medium carrot, peeled and cut into 1-inch pieces

2 cups whole wheat couscous

2 tablespoons finely chopped fresh cilantro

1. In a large skillet over medium heat, heat ¼ cup broth. Add the onion and garlic and sauté for 3 minutes. Add the coriander, cumin, turmeric, salt, and black pepper and sauté for 3 minutes.
2. Add the tomatoes and cook for 2 minutes. Put in the peas, sweet potato, carrot, and remaining ¾ cup broth.
3. Bring to a boil, lower heat, cover, and simmer for about 20 minutes, until vegetables are tender.
4. Bring 4 cups of water to a boil in a medium saucepan. Add the couscous slowly to the pot. Bring to a boil. Cover and turn off the heat. Let the couscous stand covered for 5 minutes, until water is absorbed. Fluff with a fork
5. Serve curry over cooked couscous, sprinkled with cilantro.

DID YOU KNOW?

Traditionally, couscous took quite a bit of effort to prepare, including several steaming sessions in a special multilayer pot. Lucky for us, a 5-minute version is now available in most grocery stores.

PER SERVING (⅙ OF RECIPE):		
295 calories	10.8 g protein	359 mg sodium
0.7 g fat	62.9 g carbohydrate	54 mg calcium
0.1 g saturated fat	7.5 g sugar	2.5 mg iron
2.1% calories from fat	7.9 g fiber	19.6 mg vitamin C
0 mg cholesterol		3858 mcg beta-carotene
		0.7 mg vitamin E

MULTI-MUSHROOM SAUCE

MAKES 4 SERVINGS ■ **PREPARATION TIME: 40 minutes** ■ **COOK TIME: 20 minutes**

This earthy mushroom sauce uses three different types of mushrooms for triple the flavor! It is delicious served over pasta or rice.

1½ cups dried porcini mushrooms

3 cups vegetable broth

½ cup finely chopped onion

2 cups sliced button mushroom caps

2 cups sliced cremini mushroom caps

½ teaspoon lemon zest

3 garlic cloves, minced

Kosher or sea salt to taste

Freshly ground black pepper to taste

½ cup dry red wine

1 tablespoon arrowroot

½ cup chopped fresh parsley or cilantro, for garnish

1. Combine porcini mushrooms with boiling water to cover in a medium bowl. Let stand for 30 minutes. Drain, and chop porcini mushrooms coarsely. Set aside.
2. Heat ¾ cup broth in a large skillet. Add onion and sauté for 4 minutes. Add porcini, button, and cremini mushrooms and sauté for 3 minutes. Put in the lemon zest, garlic, and salt, and black pepper and cook for 2 minutes.
3. Stir in the remaining 2¼ cups broth and red wine and bring to a boil. Cook for 3 minutes. Mix the arrowroot with 1 tablespoon water and stir until smooth. Add to the mushroom sauce and cook for 5 to 10 minutes, until the sauce thickens.
4. Garnish with parsley or cilantro before serving.

DID YOU KNOW?

Ancient hieroglyphics have led researchers to believe that Egyptians once associated mushrooms with immortality. They weren't far off—current research suggests mushroom consumption may help protect against breast cancer, and studies are under way on their effect on the immune system.

PER SERVING (¼ OF RECIPE):

103 calories	3.1 g protein	863 mg sodium
0.4 g fat	18.7 g carbohydrate	36 mg calcium
0.1 g saturated fat	6.3 g sugar	1.5 mg iron
3% calories from fat	2.7 g fiber	13.4 mg vitamin C
0 mg cholesterol		563 mcg beta-carotene
		0.1 mg vitamin E

POLENTA WITH ZESTY MUSHROOM SAUCE

MAKES 4 SERVINGS ■ **PREPARATION TIME: 15 minutes** ■ **COOK TIME: 30 to 40 minutes**

Polenta is made from cornmeal and is a tasty alternative to pasta or rice. This dish combines the smooth, creamy texture of polenta with a flavorful tomato and mushroom sauce.

2¼ cups vegetable broth

½ cup chopped red onion

3 cups thinly sliced cremini mushroom caps

2 teaspoons dried basil

2 teaspoons dried oregano

3 garlic cloves, minced

Pinch of crushed red pepper

Pinch of sugar

2 (14.5-ounce) cans diced tomatoes with Italian seasonings, with liquid

¾ cup cornmeal

Kosher or sea salt to taste

Freshly ground black pepper to taste

1. Heat ¼ cup broth in a large skillet over medium heat. Put in the onion and sauté for 4 minutes. Add the mushrooms and sauté for 3 minutes. Add the basil, oregano, garlic, crushed red pepper, and sugar and cook for 1 minute. Add the tomatoes, reduce heat to low, and simmer for 5 to 7 minutes.

2. Meanwhile, combine the remaining 2 cups broth and 1 cup water in a saucepan. Bring to a boil and stir in cornmeal. Reduce heat and simmer until thick, stirring almost constantly. Serve tomato mixture over polenta.

DID YOU KNOW?

Polenta's nickname is "Italian grits." Once considered a poor man's food in Italy, it is now gaining the recognition it deserves. Try grilling the already prepared polenta or using it as a base like bread for bruschetta.

PER SERVING (¼ OF RECIPE):

180 calories	5.6 g protein	979 mg sodium
1 g fat	39 g carbohydrate	103 mg calcium
0.1 g saturated fat	8.9 g sugar	4 mg iron
4.6% calories from fat	4.2 g fiber	21.3 mg vitamin C
0 mg cholesterol		357 mcg beta-carotene
		1.6 mg vitamin E

PRETTY STUFFED PEPPERS

MAKES 4 SERVINGS ■ PREPARATION TIME: 15 minutes ■ COOK TIME: 30 minutes

A festive addition to a table, these bright vibrant peppers will have you shouting olé!

1 cup short- or long-grain brown rice

4 medium red bell peppers

2 medium yellow bell peppers

¼ cup vegetable broth

1 cup chopped onion

1 teaspoon chili powder

1 teaspoon ground cumin

1 teaspoon dried oregano

¼ teaspoon sea salt

¼ teaspoon ground black pepper

1 (15-ounce) can black beans, drained and rinsed

1 cup seeded and chopped tomato

8 slices Cheddar-style soy or rice cheese

1. Preheat the oven to 400°F.
2. Bring 2 cups of water to a boil in a medium saucepan. Slowly add the rice to the pot, stir once, cover and simmer the rice on low heat for 40 to 45 minutes or until rice is tender. Do not stir while the rice is cooking.
3. Cut each bell pepper in half lengthwise. Remove seeds and ribs. Bring a large saucepan of water to a boil. Add the bell pepper halves and blanch for about 4 minutes. Drain and pat dry.
4. Heat the broth in a skillet over medium heat. Add the onion and sauté for about 3 minutes. Add chili powder, cumin, oregano, salt, and black pepper. Sauté for 1 minute. Add the beans, rice, and tomato and sauté for 2 minutes.
5. Stuff bell peppers with the mixture, packing them well. Top each bell pepper with a slice of cheese. Place in an 8 x 8-inch baking dish.
6. Bake bell peppers, uncovered, for about 20 minutes. Set oven to broil. Broil bell peppers for 1 to 2 minutes, until the top is browned and cheese is bubbly.

DID YOU KNOW?

The longer a bell pepper ripens, the sweeter it becomes. A red bell pepper supplies nearly eight times the beta-carotene of a green bell pepper. And ounce for ounce, yellow, red, or orange bell peppers can contain upward of four times the vitamin C as an orange.

PER SERVING (¼ OF RECIPE):

425 calories	21.2 g protein	787 mg sodium
8.5 g fat	69.1 g carbohydrate	135 mg calcium
1.4 g saturated fat	10.7 g sugar	4.1 mg iron
17.1% calories from fat	15.6 g fiber	195.8 mg vitamin C
0 mg cholesterol		1169 mcg beta-carotene
		2.1 mg vitamin E

QUINOA TIMBALES

MAKES FOUR 1-CUP SERVINGS ■ PREPARATION TIME: 10 minutes ■ COOK TIME: 20 minutes

Presenting this dish as individual timbales will add a touch of elegance to your dinner party. If you don't have ramekins, try using a measuring cup to form the timbales.

¼ cup short-grain brown rice

1 cup quinoa

2 cups vegetable broth

½ cup cooked or canned adzuki beans, French lentils, or small white beans

½ cup finely chopped fresh parsley

2 garlic cloves, minced

1 teaspoon grated lemon zest

Kosher or sea salt to taste

Freshly ground black pepper to taste

8 strips roasted red bell pepper, for garnish

4 parsley sprigs, for garnish

1. Bring ½ cup water to a boil in a small saucepan. Slowly add the rice, bring to a boil. Cover, and simmer on low heat for about 30 minutes or until rice is tender.

2. Rinse quinoa in a fine sieve under running water for about 1 minute. Bring the broth to a boil over high heat. Add the quinoa and bring to another boil. Lower heat, cover, and simmer for 15 minutes.

3. Add the beans, cooked rice, parsley, garlic, lemon zest, salt, and black pepper.

4. Pack the quinoa into four ramekin dishes. Turn the ramekins upside down onto each plate and twist and lift the ramekin. Top each timbale with strips of roasted bell pepper and a parsley sprig.

DID YOU KNOW?

You can use your rice cooker to cook quinoa. Just use the water and cook time settings for regular white rice.

PER SERVING (¼ OF RECIPE):

249 calories	9.6 g protein	633 mg sodium
3 g fat	46.3 g carbohydrate	54 mg calcium
0.4 g saturated fat	4.7 g sugar	3.3 mg iron
10.9% calories from fat	6.8 g fiber	21.4 mg vitamin C
0 mg cholesterol		635 mcg beta-carotene
		1.2 mg vitamin E

SPRINGTIME ASPARAGUS AND TOFU STIR-FRY

MAKES 4 SERVINGS ■ **PREPARATION TIME: 10 minutes** ■ **COOK TIME: 25 minutes**

This light stir-fry makes a quick and tasty meal. Be sure to save some for lunch the next day.

1 cup quinoa

1½ cups vegetable broth

1 medium onion, thinly sliced

5 garlic cloves, minced

2 tablespoons minced fresh ginger

¾ pound asparagus, ends trimmed, diagonally sliced into 1-inch pieces

3 large carrots, julienned

8 ounces extra-firm tofu, drained, patted dry, and cut into 1-inch cubes

1 tablespoon reduced-sodium soy sauce

2 teaspoons rice vinegar or rice wine

1. Rinse quinoa in a fine sieve under running water for 1 minute. Bring 1 cup water to a boil in a medium saucepan. Add quinoa, lower heat, and simmer, covered, for about 15 minutes. Set aside.

2. Meanwhile, heat ½ cup broth in a wok or heavy skillet over medium-high heat. Put in the onion, garlic, and ginger and stir-fry for 3 minutes. Add the asparagus and carrots and stir-fry for 1 minute. Add the remaining 1 cup broth, cover, and steam for 3 minutes until carrots are bright orange and asparagus is bright green and crisp. Add the tofu.

3. Serve stir-fried mixture over quinoa and drizzle with soy sauce and rice vinegar or rice wine.

DID YOU KNOW?

Asparagus is great source of folic acid, providing two-thirds of the daily value in one cup. Folic acid, or folate, helps protect against heart disease, cancer, and neural tube defects in the fetus.

PER SERVING (¼ OF RECIPE):

260 calories	13.8 g protein	537 mg sodium
6.2 g fat	39.8 g carbohydrate	165 mg calcium
0.7 g saturated fat	7.3 g sugar	3.8 mg iron
20.5% calories from fat	6 g fiber	7.9 mg vitamin C
0 mg cholesterol		4473 mcg beta-carotene
		2.2 mg vitamin E

STUFFED PORTOBELLO MUSHROOMS
WITH BROWN RICE AND TOMATOES

MAKES 4 STUFFED MUSHROOMS ■ PREPARATION TIME: 20 minutes ■ COOK TIME: 1 hour

This hearty dish is a delicious blend of earthy mushroom texture and spicy flavors.

2 cups vegetable broth

1 cup short-grain brown rice, rinsed

¼ cup finely chopped onion

½ cup finely chopped carrot

1 teaspoon dried basil

½ teaspoon dried oregano

½ cup chopped red tomato

½ cup chopped yellow tomato

3 tablespoons finely chopped fresh parsley

1 tablespoon chopped fresh chives

Kosher or sea salt to taste

Freshly ground black pepper to taste

4 portobello mushroom caps

Vegetable oil cooking spray

¼ cup vegan Parmesan cheese

1. Bring broth to a boil in a medium saucepan. Add rinsed rice and bring to another boil. Lower heat, cover, and simmer for about 45 minutes. During the last 5 minutes of cooking time, add onion, carrot, basil, and oregano.

2. In a bowl, combine cooked rice, tomatoes, parsley, chives, salt, and black pepper. Set aside. Preheat the oven broiler.

3. Remove the gills from the undersides of the mushrooms using a spoon; discard gills. Place the mushrooms, gill-side down, on a foil-lined broiler tray that has been coated with cooking spray. Broil mushrooms for about 5 minutes.

4. Turn mushrooms over and stuff each mushroom with equal amounts of the rice mixture. Sprinkle each with vegan Parmesan. Broil mushrooms for about 5 to 6 minutes, until lightly browned.

DID YOU KNOW?

Mushrooms are a low-calorie source of B vitamins. Portobellos are delicious whether stuffed, served on a bun, or used to top salads.

PER STUFFED MUSHROOM:

230 calories	8.6 g protein	715 mg sodium
2.9 g fat	44 g carbohydrate	47 mg calcium
0.5 g saturated fat	3.8 g sugar	1.7 mg iron
10.8% calories from fat	7.5 g fiber	13.5 mg vitamin C
0 mg cholesterol		1626 mcg beta-carotene
		0.5 mg vitamin E

TRINIDADIAN CURRIED CAULIFLOWER, POTATOES, AND PEAS

MAKES FOUR 1-CUP SERVINGS ■ **PREPARATION TIME: 20 minutes** ■ **COOK TIME: 45 minutes**

If you enjoy vegetable samosas, you will adore this dish. It has all the flavor and little fat.

¼ cup vegetable broth

1 large onion, chopped

4 garlic cloves, minced

2 tablespoons minced fresh ginger

1 habanero or jalapeño pepper, chopped

⅔ cup canned tomato purée

½ cup raisins

1 teaspoon ground coriander

1 teaspoon ground cumin

¼ teaspoon turmeric

¼ cup chopped fresh cilantro

1 tablespoon reduced-sodium soy sauce

2 small sweet potatoes, peeled and cut into ½-inch cubes

½ head cauliflower, separated into florets

2 cups fresh or frozen green peas, thawed

1. Heat broth in a large skillet over medium heat. Put in the onion, garlic, ginger, and hot pepper. Sauté for 5 to 6 minutes. Stir in 3 tablespoons water and cook for 3 minutes.

2. Stir in tomato purée, raisins, coriander, cumin, turmeric, cilantro, soy sauce, and sweet potatoes. Cook for 15 minutes.

3. Add the cauliflower, cover, and simmer for 15 to 20 minutes. Add peas and cook for 5 additional minutes.

DID YOU KNOW?

This recipe is similar to aloo gobi, a dish commonly found in Indian restaurants. *Aloo* means "potato" and *gobi* means "cauliflower."

PER SERVING (¼ OF RECIPE):

205 calories	8 g protein	385 mg sodium
1 g fat	45.3 g carbohydrate	80 mg calcium
0.1 g saturated fat	22.5 g sugar	3.5 mg iron
4% calories from fat	8.7 g fiber	70.6 mg vitamin C
0 mg cholesterol		4172 mcg beta-carotene
		1.4 mg vitamin E

ZUPPA DI LENTICCHIE

MAKES FOUR 1-CUP SERVINGS ■ **PREPARATION TIME: 35 minutes** ■ **COOK TIME: 30 minutes**

Italian lore says that lentils served on New Year's Day bring good luck all year long.

½ cup chopped onion

4¼ cups vegetable broth

2 garlic cloves, finely chopped

¾ cup dried brown lentils

1 tablespoon fresh thyme leaves

½ teaspoon freshly ground black pepper

¼ cup elbow macaroni

4 slices whole-grain bread, toasted

1. In a large saucepan, sauté the onion in ¼ cup broth over medium heat until soft. Add the garlic and sauté for another minute.
2. Add the remaining 4 cups broth and bring to a simmer.
3. Add the lentils and thyme and bring broth back to a simmer. Cover and simmer for 15 minutes.
4. Add black pepper and pasta and simmer for an additional 8 minutes.
5. To serve, top each bowl of soup with a slice of bread.

DID YOU KNOW?

Packed with iron, protein, fiber, vitamins, and minerals, lentils are a popular dietary staple in many countries.

PER SERVING (¼ OF RECIPE):

243 calories	14.3 g protein	1136 mg sodium
1.6 g fat	44.3 g carbohydrate	67 mg calcium
0.3 g saturated fat	7.2 g sugar	4.5 mg iron
5.7% calories from fat	8.6 g fiber	4.1 mg vitamin C
0 mg cholesterol		282 mcg beta-carotene
		0.3 mg vitamin E

SPICED SQUASH BISQUE *low carb*

MAKES SIX 1-CUP SERVINGS ■ **PREPARATION TIME: 30 minutes** ■ **COOK TIME: 50 minutes**

This flavorful bisque will fill your home with an inviting holiday aroma.

4½ cups peeled, seeded, and cubed winter squash

1 cup chopped onion

3¼ cups vegetable broth

2 garlic cloves, minced

1 teaspoon ground cardamom

1½ teaspoons ground cumin

¼ teaspoon ground nutmeg

¼ teaspoon cayenne pepper, or to taste

1 teaspoon salt

¾ cup dairy-free sour cream, to garnish (optional)

1. Preheat the oven to 375°F.
2. Place squash in a baking dish and bake for 30 minutes, or until tender. Set aside.
3. In a large stockpot, sauté the onion in ¼ cup broth over medium heat until translucent, about 3 minutes. Add garlic, cardamom, cumin, nutmeg, cayenne, and salt. Sauté for 2 to 3 minutes. Put in the cooked squash. Add the remaining 3 cups broth.
4. Purée the soup in batches in a food processor or blender until smooth.
5. Return soup to pot and bring to a boil. Turn down to simmer, partially cover pot, and simmer for 10 minutes or until heated thoroughly.
6. If using, garnish the top of each bowl of soup with 2 tablespoons dairy-free sour cream.

DID YOU KNOW?

You can use any type of winter squash in this recipe. A favorite combination is hubbard squash, acorn squash, and butternut squash. Some winter squashes require a longer cooking time, so be sure to check tenderness with a fork.

PER SERVING (⅙ OF RECIPE):

158 calories	1.3 g protein	908 mg sodium
0.3 g fat	14.3 g carbohydrate	53 mg calcium
0.1 g saturated fat	6.2 g sugar	1 mg iron
4.5 % calories from fat	1.8 g fiber	15.5 mg vitamin C
0 mg cholesterol		4298 mcg beta-carotene
		1.2 mg vitamin E

MOROCCAN-STYLE PILAF

This dish is a crowd favorite, with delicious Moroccan flavors and spices.

4¼ cups vegetable broth

1 medium onion, chopped

2 garlic cloves, minced

1 large carrot, chopped

2 cups long-grain brown rice, rinsed in a fine sieve for 1 minute

1 large pinch saffron

1 cup canned chickpeas, drained and rinsed

½ cup chopped dried apricots

¼ cup raisins (optional)

2 teaspoons fresh lemon juice

2 tablespoons minced fresh parsley

Kosher or sea salt to taste

Freshly ground black pepper to taste

1. Heat ¼ cup broth in a large saucepan over medium heat. Put in the onion, garlic, and carrot and sauté for 5 minutes. Add the rice and sauté for 2 minutes.

2. Dissolve saffron in the remaining 4 cups broth. Add the broth to rice and bring to a boil. Lower heat and simmer for about 50 minutes. Add the chickpeas, apricots, and raisins, if using. Cover and cook for 5 minutes. Add lemon juice, parsley, salt, and black pepper.

DID YOU KNOW?

Saffron adds a beautiful golden color to the dish. But be careful: a little goes a long way; adding too much can give a metallic taste. Saffron is the most expensive spice in the world. Some people use turmeric as a less expensive alternative.

PER SERVING (¼ OF RECIPE):

483 calories	12.8 g protein	1206 mg sodium
4.1 g fat	100.5 g carbohydrate	82 mg calcium
0.7 g saturated fat	14.7 g sugar	3.2 mg iron
7% calories from fat	15 g fiber	6.4 mg vitamin C
0 mg cholesterol		2087 mcg beta-carotene
		1.2 mg vitamin E

THREE-LAYER TORTILLA CASSEROLE

MAKES 4 SERVINGS ■ **PREPARATION TIME: 30 minutes** ■ **COOK TIME: 30 minutes**

This Mexican-inspired dish can be mild or spicy, depending on the salsa you choose. If you prefer, use corn tortillas rather than whole wheat.

Vegetable oil cooking spray

1 (15-ounce) can black beans, drained and rinsed

½ cup vegetable broth

2 garlic cloves, minced

1 teaspoon dried oregano

¼ teaspoon cayenne pepper

1 large red onion, chopped

2 cups chopped zucchini

1 cup frozen corn, thawed

1 teaspoon ground cumin

2 tablespoons minced fresh cilantro

Kosher or sea salt to taste

Freshly ground black pepper to taste

3 (8-inch) whole wheat tortillas

¾ cup prepared chunky salsa

1. Preheat the oven to 350°F. Coat a 10-inch pie plate with cooking spray and set aside.

2. Add the beans, ¼ cup broth, garlic, oregano, and cayenne to a food processor or blender and blend until smooth but thick. Set aside.

3. Heat the remaining ¼ cup broth in a large skillet over medium heat. Add the onion and sauté for 5 minutes. Put in the zucchini and corn and sauté for 3 minutes. Add the cumin and cilantro and sauté for 1 minute. Season with salt and black pepper.

4. Place one tortilla in the prepared pie plate. Spread about one-third of the bean mixture over the tortilla. Using a slotted spoon, add one-third of the vegetable mixture on top of the beans. Add one-third of the salsa over the vegetables and top with another tortilla. Make two more layers in the same fashion, to make a total of three layers.

5. Bake uncovered for about 30 minutes. Cut into wedges to serve.

DID YOU KNOW?

This dish uses the corn, beans, and squash, known to Native Americans as Three Sisters. These three plants complement one another in the garden. Beans pull nitrogen into the soil, nitrogen helps corn grow, while squash's broad sheltering leaves make it hard for weeds to grow and its spiny vines repel predators. On your plate, they create a perfect nutritional balance of carbohydrates, protein, fiber, and vitamins.

PER SERVING (¼ OF RECIPE):

243 calories	11.2 g protein	841 mg sodium
2 g fat	49.5 g carbohydrate	98 mg calcium
0.4 g saturated fat	6 g sugar	3.6 mg iron
6.9% calories from fat	13 g fiber	7.9 mg vitamin C
0 mg cholesterol		546 mcg beta-carotene
		1 mg vitamin E

BROWN RICE, CHICKPEA, AND VEGETABLE SOUP

MAKES 6 SERVINGS ■ **PREPARATION TIME: 10 minutes** ■ **COOK TIME: 25 to 30 minutes**

Quick-cooking brown rice is ready in just 10 minutes, making this hearty soup a quick and easy option for lunch or dinner.

5 cups vegetable broth

½ cup quick-cooking brown rice

1 (15-ounce) can chickpeas, drained and rinsed

1 medium carrot, chopped

½ cup small cauliflower florets

½ cup small broccoli florets

1 (15-ounce) can chopped tomatoes

2 teaspoons dried basil

1 teaspoon dried oregano

Kosher or sea salt to taste

Freshly ground black pepper to taste

1. Bring the broth to a boil in a large saucepan,. Add chickpeas, carrot, cauliflower, broccoli, tomatoes, basil, and oregano and simmer for 15 to 20 minutes.

2. Add the brown rice. Cover, reduce heat to low, and cook for 10 minutes. Season with salt and black pepper.

DID YOU KNOW?

Quick-cooking brown rice is parboiled and then dehydrated for packaging. The parboiling opens the outer husk, making the grains more porous and allows the water to be absorbed quickly when it is cooked. As a result, it is lighter in color and has a fluffier texture than regular brown rice.

PER SERVING (⅙ OF RECIPE):

167 calories	6.6 g protein	1080 mg sodium
1.9 g fat	32.4 g carbohydrate	71 mg calcium
0.3 g saturated fat	5 g sugar	2.6 mg iron
9.6% calories from fat	6.3 g fiber	16.2 mg vitamin C
0 mg cholesterol		1125 mcg beta-carotene
		1 mg vitamin E

GARLICKY PINTO BEAN AND PASTA BAKE

MAKES SIX 1-CUP SERVINGS ■ **PREPARATION TIME: 15 minutes** ■ **COOK TIME: 25 minutes**

This warm casserole combines pasta and chili in one meal. Kids love it as a chili mac.

½ cup vegetable broth

1 large onion, chopped

5 garlic cloves, thinly sliced

1 tablespoon chili powder

1 teaspoon dried oregano

¼ teaspoon cayenne pepper

2 (14.5-ounce) cans diced tomatoes, with liquid

1 cup whole wheat pasta shells or elbow macaroni

2 (15-ounce) cans pinto beans, drained and rinsed

1 cup broken baked tortilla chips

1. Preheat the oven to 325°F.
2. Heat the broth in a large skillet over medium heat. Add the onion and garlic and sauté for 5 minutes. Add the chili powder, oregano, and cayenne. Cook for 1 minute.
3. Add the tomatoes and bring to a boil. Put in the pasta and cook for 15 minutes until pasta is cooked through. Stir in beans. Transfer the mixture to a casserole dish. Top casserole with corn chips.
4. Bake, uncovered, for about 10 minutes.

DID YOU KNOW?

An easy way to peel garlic is to smash it first with the flat side of a chopping knife. The garlic pops open, and the peel comes off with ease.

PER SERVING (⅙ OF RECIPE):

298 calories	14.3 g protein	419 mg sodium
2.5 g fat	58.7 g carbohydrate	112 mg calcium
0.4 g saturated fat	5.5 g sugar	4.8 mg iron
7.2% calories from fat	13.3 g fiber	16.4 mg vitamin C
0 mg cholesterol		338 mcg beta-carotene
		2.6 mg vitamin E

SPICY RED BEANS AND BROWN RICE

MAKES SIX 1-CUP SERVINGS ■ PREPARATION TIME: 15 minutes ■ COOK TIME: 1 hour

This soul-warming dish is a cinch. Chipotle peppers give it a Southern flare. If you make a bit extra, you'll have the filling on hand for an easy burrito.

3¼ cups vegetable broth

1 onion, chopped

2 garlic cloves, minced

1½ cups long-grain brown rice, rinsed

1 (14.5-ounce) can diced tomatoes, with liquid

1 teaspoon chopped canned chipotle pepper in adobo sauce

1 (15-ounce) can red kidney beans, drained

Sea salt to taste

Freshly ground black pepper to taste

1. Heat ¼ cup broth in a large saucepan over medium heat. Put in the onion and garlic and sauté for 3 minutes. Add the brown rice and sauté for 2 minutes.

2. Add the remaining 3 cups broth, tomatoes, and chipotle pepper and bring to a boil. Lower heat and simmer for about 45 minutes, until the rice is cooked through. Add beans and cook for 2 minutes. Season with salt and black pepper.

DID YOU KNOW?

Red beans and rice is a symbolic dish of Louisiana Creole cuisine, traditionally made on Mondays, with red beans spooned over rice and often served with a bottle of hot sauce. The combination of rice and beans provides a good balance of all the essential amino acids that make a complete protein.

PER SERVING (⅙ OF RECIPE):

260 calories	9 g protein	882 mg sodium
1.8 g fat	53 g carbohydrate	63 mg calcium
0.3 g saturated fat	4.9 g sugar	2.5 mg iron
5.7% calories from fat	9.2 g fiber	8.5 mg vitamin C
0 mg cholesterol		212 mcg beta-carotene
		0.6 mg vitamin E

STUFFED POBLANO PEPPERS with ENCHILADA SAUCE

MAKES 4 SERVINGS ■ PREPARATION TIME: 15 minutes ■ COOK TIME: 15 minutes

This dish is a flavorful new twist on stuffed peppers.

¼ cup vegetable broth

½ red onion, chopped

2 garlic cloves, minced

½ teaspoon ground cumin

½ teaspoon dried oregano

Sea salt to taste

½ cup instant polenta

1 (10-ounce) package frozen corn, thawed and drained

3 scallions, finely chopped

4 poblano peppers, halved lengthwise and seeded

2 cups prepared enchilada sauce

1. Preheat the oven to 400°F.
2. Heat the broth in a large skillet over medium heat. Put in the onion and garlic and sauté for 3 minutes. Add the cumin and oregano and sauté for 1 minute. Set aside.
3. In a medium saucepan, bring 2¼ cups water to a boil. Add salt. Gradually whisk in polenta. Cook for about 4 minutes, stirring constantly. Stir in corn and scallions.
4. Mix onion mixture into polenta. Divide polenta mixture among poblano pepper halves. Pour about 1 cup enchilada sauce into the bottom of a 9 x 13-inch pan. Set poblano peppers on top of sauce. Cover with the remaining 1 cup sauce, and bake uncovered for about 10 minutes.

DID YOU KNOW?

The poblano is a mild chile pepper, slightly spicier than a bell pepper.

PER SERVING (¼ OF RECIPE):

166 calories	6.4 g protein	1129 mg sodium
1 g fat	38.7 g carbohydrate	112 mg calcium
0.1 g saturated fat	10.8 g sugar	5.6 mg iron
5.1% calories from fat	5.6 g fiber	113.8 mg vitamin C
0 mg cholesterol		700 mcg beta-carotene
		2.2 mg vitamin E

SWEET POTATO AND GREEN PEA CURRY OVER BROWN RICE

MAKES FOUR 1-CUP SERVINGS ■ **PREPARATION TIME: 10 minutes** ■ **COOK TIME: 30 minutes**

This curry is a colorful and fragrant topping for brown rice. Feel free to add a little more vegetable broth for a lighter consistency. If you like, try broccoli florets or carrots instead of peas.

1 cup long-grain brown rice

1 teaspoon cumin seeds

1 teaspoon coriander seeds

2¾ cups vegetable broth

¼ cup chopped onion

2 garlic cloves, minced

2 small sweet potatoes, peeled and cut into ½-inch cubes

1 teaspoon turmeric

2 teaspoons fresh lemon zest

1 (10-ounce) package frozen baby green peas, thawed

2 tablespoons chopped fresh cilantro

Sea salt to taste

Freshly ground black pepper to taste

1. Bring 2 cups of water to a boil in a medium saucepan. Slowly add the rice, bring to a boil, cover, and simmer on low heat for about 40 to 45 minutes or until rice is tender. Set aside.
2. In a small dry skillet, place cumin and coriander seeds and shake over medium heat until fragrant.
3. Place seeds in a spice grinder and grind until fine. Set aside.
4. Heat ¼ cup broth in a large saucepan. Add the onion and garlic and cook for 2 minutes. Put in the sweet potatoes, turmeric, and ground cumin and coriander. Cook for 2 minutes. Add the remaining 2½ cups broth and bring to a boil. Cover and lower heat to medium-low. Cook mixture until the potatoes are tender, about 12 to 15 minutes. Add lemon zest and peas. Cook, uncovered, for 3 minutes. Add cilantro, salt, and black pepper. Serve over rice.

DID YOU KNOW?

Cumin and coriander are often used in curry dishes. Toasting the seeds before grinding them brings out their natural oils. To make sure that you don't burn them, pay attention to the smell—once you can smell the fragrant aroma, the spices are ready. If you don't have a spice grinder, a mortar and pestle work almost as well.

PER SERVING (¼ OF RECIPE):

270 calories	8.2 g protein	857 mg sodium
1.9 g fat	55.8 g carbohydrate	60 mg calcium
0.4 g saturated fat	8 g sugar	2.6 mg iron
5.9% calories from fat	9 g fiber	13.8 mg vitamin C
0 mg cholesterol		4559 mcg beta-carotene
		0.5 mg vitamin E

BAKED GREAT NORTHERN BEANS WITH CHILES

MAKES FOUR ¾-CUP SERVINGS ■ PREPARATION TIME: 10 minutes ■ COOK TIME: 30 minutes

A little sweet paired with a little spice, these baked beans are a breeze to make and a joy to eat.

2 (15-ounce) cans great northern beans, drained and rinsed

1 medium onion, chopped

2 garlic cloves, minced

3 tablespoons canned chopped green chiles, or 1 small fresh jalapeño pepper, seeds removed and finely chopped

1 (10-ounce) can diced tomatoes, with liquid

2 tablespoons apple cider vinegar

1 tablespoon light agave nectar

1 teaspoon chili powder

½ teaspoon dry mustard

Kosher or sea salt to taste

Freshly ground black pepper to taste

1. Preheat the oven to 350°F. Combine all ingredients in a 1-quart casserole dish. Cover and bake for 30 minutes.
2. Uncover and bake for an additional 20 to 30 minutes.

DID YOU KNOW?

Great northern beans are different from cannellini and navy beans, and are like small white lima beans, with a nutty flavor.

PER SERVING (¼ OF RECIPE):

247 calories	15.2 g protein	511 mg sodium
0.9 g fat	46.8 g carbohydrate	177 mg calcium
0.2 g saturated fat	7 g sugar	6.6 mg iron
2.9% calories from fat	10.5 g fiber	11 mg vitamin C
0 mg cholesterol		149 mcg beta-carotene
		0.1 mg vitamin E

VEGETABLE PAELLA

MAKES SIX 1-CUP SERVINGS ■ **PREPARATION TIME: 15 minutes** ■ **COOK TIME: 50 minutes**

Although paella is traditionally made with shellfish, this vegan version is healthier and more flavorful. You can make a big batch and enjoy it for days.

3½ cups vegetable broth

1 large onion, chopped

2 garlic cloves, chopped

1 medium green or red bell pepper, seeded and chopped

1½ cups short-grain brown rice

1 teaspoon saffron

¼ teaspoon crushed red pepper

1 (15-ounce) can artichoke hearts, drained, or 1 (8-ounce) package frozen artichoke hearts

1 cup fresh or frozen green peas

1 (15-ounce) can kidney beans, drained

Kosher or sea salt to taste

Freshly ground black pepper to taste

1. Heat ½ cup broth in a heavy skillet over medium-high heat. Add the onion, garlic, bell pepper, and rice and sauté for 5 minutes.
2. Add remaining 3 cups broth, saffron, and crushed red pepper. Bring to a boil, cover, and cook over low heat for 45 minutes. Add the artichoke hearts, peas, and beans. Cover and cook for an additional 10 minutes, until rice is tender. Season with salt and black pepper.

DID YOU KNOW?

The word *paella* is derived from the Latin word *patella*, which means "pan." Paella is commonly cooked in a shallow pan and is traditionally eaten straight from the patella. You can find paella cooking pans at your local specialty cooking store.

PER SERVING (⅙ OF RECIPE):

302 calories	11.4 g protein	945 mg sodium
2 g fat	61.7 g carbohydrate	61 mg calcium
0.4 g saturated fat	6.1 g sugar	2.6 mg iron
5.4% calories from fat	14.3 g fiber	23.3 mg vitamin C
0 mg cholesterol		315 mcg beta-carotene
		0.3 mg vitamin E

GINGER TOFU *low carb*

MAKES 4 SERVINGS ■ PREPARATION TIME: 10 minutes ■ COOK TIME: 10 minutes

This is a simple, quick dish great for last-minute meals. Serve it over brown rice, and, if you like, add any vegetable you have on hand.

¼ cup plus ⅔ cup vegetable broth

1 (16-ounce) package extra-firm tofu, pressed and cut into 1-inch triangles

¼ cup hoisin sauce

1 tablespoon dry sherry

1 teaspoon arrowroot

2 teaspoons reduced-sodium soy sauce

1 teaspoon agave nectar

⅛ teaspoon crushed red pepper

2 teaspoons grated fresh ginger

2 garlic cloves, minced

1. Heat ¼ cup broth in a large nonstick skillet over medium-high heat. Add tofu (in batches if necessary) and sauté on both sides for about 3 minutes per side. Remove from skillet.

2. In a bowl, combine the remaining ⅔ cup broth, hoisin sauce, sherry, arrowroot, soy sauce, agave nectar, and crushed red pepper. Mix well.

3. Add ginger and garlic to the skillet and sauté for 30 seconds. Add broth mixture and cook 1 minute. Add tofu to skillet and coat tofu with sauce.

DID YOU KNOW?

You'll find fresh ginger in the produce section. Peel off the tough outer skin, then grate or chop. It has a wonderful aroma and is a great addition to many dishes.

PER SERVING (¼ OF RECIPE):

159 calories	12 g protein	573 mg sodium
7.2 g fat	13.3 g carbohydrate	212 mg calcium
0.7 g saturated fat	3 g sugar	2.4 mg iron
38.1% calories from fat	1 g fiber	1.2 mg vitamin C
0 mg cholesterol		63 mcg beta-carotene
		0.1 mg vitamin E

BLACK-EYED PEA AND BROWN RICE PILAF WITH BROWNED ONIONS

MAKES 4 SERVINGS ■ PREPARATION TIME: 5 minutes ■ COOK TIME: 75 minutes

The browned onions in this recipe are flavorful and light, because they are oil-free.

1½ cups long-grain brown rice, rinsed

1½ cups vegetable broth

2 large onions, halved and thinly sliced

1 (15-ounce) can black-eyed peas, drained and rinsed, or 2 cups frozen black-eyed peas, thawed

Sea salt to taste

Freshly ground black pepper to taste

2 drops Tabasco sauce

1. Bring rice and 3 cups water to a boil in a large saucepan. Cover, lower heat, and simmer for about 45 minutes, until the water has been absorbed and the rice is cooked. Set aside.

2. Heat ½ cup broth in a large skillet over medium heat. Add onions and cook, stirring frequently, for about 10 minutes. Add another ½ cup broth and continue to cook and stir for 10 minutes. Add remaining ½ cup broth and continue to stir for another 10 minutes, until onions are browned and soft.

3. Add black-eyed peas to onions and season with salt, black pepper, and Tabasco sauce. Serve over rice.

DID YOU KNOW?

Black-eyed peas are a popular food served on New Year's Day as they have long been thought to bring good luck.

PER SERVING (¼ OF RECIPE):

375 calories	12.5 g protein	694 mg sodium
2.6 g fat	76.1 g carbohydrate	63 mg calcium
0.5 g saturated fat	5.2 g sugar	3 mg iron
5.8% calories from fat	12 g fiber	3.7 mg vitamin C
0 mg cholesterol		99 mcg beta-carotene
		0.3 mg vitamin E

STUFFED CABBAGE

MAKES 8 SERVINGS ■ **PREPARATION TIME: 5 minutes** ■ **COOK TIME: 45 minutes**

This dish is the ultimate comfort food and perfect for holiday gatherings. Walnuts offer texture, while the tomato and spices bring it all together. If you like, substitute collard greens for cabbage.

1 onion, chopped

¼ cup vegetable broth

4 garlic cloves, minced

½ teaspoon cumin seeds

½ teaspoon black pepper

1 teaspoon coriander seeds

¼ cup tomato paste

½ cup crushed walnuts

½ cup dried brown lentils

½ cup long-grain brown rice

¾ teaspoon salt

1 small head green cabbage

1. Over medium heat, sauté onion in a saucepan with broth until onion browns. Add garlic, cumin, black pepper, and coriander and sauté for 2 minutes. Add the tomato paste and sauté for another 3 minutes, stirring the whole time. Stir in 2 cups water until well mixed and bring to a boil.

2. Add the walnuts, lentils, and rice. Cover, allow water to boil again, and then reduce heat to low. Cook for 20 minutes.

3. While lentils and rice are cooking, tear the leaves off of the cabbage and steam them until they are soft, about 20 minutes.

4. Stuff cabbage leaves with lentil and rice mixture, rolling the leaves closed and then folding the sides over.

DID YOU KNOW?

Red cabbage gets its color from pigments called anthocyanins, which not only add color, but may also help protect against cancer. Additional benefits of red cabbage include a higher concentration in vitamins A and C, compared with green cabbage.

PER SERVING (⅛ OF RECIPE):

150 calories	6.5 g protein	328 mg sodium
3.9 g fat	24.5 g carbohydrate	70 mg calcium
0.4 g saturated fat	4.4 g sugar	2 mg iron
21.9% calories from fat	5.9 g fiber	35.7 mg vitamin C
0 mg cholesterol		126 mcg beta-carotene
		0.6 mg vitamin E

CINCO DE MAYO BLACK BEANS AND RICE

MAKES 4 SERVINGS ■ **PREPARATION TIME: 10 minutes** ■ **COOK TIME: 50 minutes**

This simple dish has all the makings of a new favorite. Try it as a burrito filling or on a bed of tortilla chips.

1⅔ cups vegetable broth

¼ cup finely chopped shallots

2 teaspoons minced garlic

⅔ cup brown rice, rinsed

¼ teaspoon ground cumin

2 tablespoons finely chopped fresh cilantro

2 tablespoons finely chopped scallions

1 (15-ounce) can black beans, drained and rinsed

Kosher or sea salt to taste

Ground black pepper to taste

1. Heat ⅓ cup broth in a large saucepan over medium heat. Add shallots and garlic and sauté for 3 minutes. Add rice and cumin and sauté for 2 minutes.

2. Add remaining 1⅓ cups broth and bring to a boil. Cover and simmer on low heat for about 45 minutes, or until rice is tender. Add cilantro, scallions, beans, salt, and black pepper and mix well.

DID YOU KNOW?

You can easily cook beans from scratch. Just soak dried beans overnight (or longer). While soaking, rinse the beans once or twice and cover with clean water. Then cook them until very soft.

PER SERVING (¼ OF RECIPE):

232 calories	9.1 g protein	685 mg sodium
1.4 g fat	46.4 g carbohydrate	73 mg calcium
0.3 g saturated fat	2.3 g sugar	2.5 mg iron
5.2% calories from fat	11.4 g fiber	2.7 mg vitamin C
0 mg cholesterol		212 mcg beta-carotene
		0.1 mg vitamin E

PAN-GRILLED TOFU STEAKS
WITH SPICED TOMATO SAUCE *low carb*

MAKES 4 SERVINGS ■ PREPARATION TIME: 15 minutes ■ COOK TIME: 25 minutes

This recipe can be served hot or cold; serving it cold allows you to make everything ahead of time. The spiced tomato sauce can also be used for pasta, polenta, or pizza.

¼ cup vegetable broth

3 garlic cloves, minced

½ cup finely chopped onion

⅓ cup chopped carrot

¼ teaspoon crushed red pepper

2 cups canned whole tomatoes, with liquid, coarsely crushed

Pinch of sugar

3 tablespoons finely chopped fresh parsley

2 tablespoon finely chopped fresh basil

Kosher or sea salt to taste

Freshly ground black pepper to taste

Vegetable oil cooking spray

1 (16-ounce) package extra-firm tofu, drained and cut lengthwise into 4 slices

1. Heat broth in a medium skillet over medium-high heat. Add garlic, onion, and carrot and sauté for about 5 minutes. Add crushed red pepper and sauté for 1 minute.

2. Add tomatoes and bring to a boil. Add sugar, lower heat, and simmer for 10 minutes. Add parsley, basil, salt, and black pepper. Set aside and keep warm.

3. Heat another skillet coated with cooking spray. Add tofu and cook for about 3 to 4 minutes per side until lightly browned. Serve tofu with sauce.

DID YOU KNOW?

Tofu, or soybean curd, was first used in China around 200 BC. Firm tofu is best for stir-frying or grilling. Soft tofu works great in blended dishes or soups. Silken tofu has a creamy consistency that is perfect for puréed dishes and smoothies.

PER SERVING (¼ OF RECIPE):

141 calories	12.8 g protein	396 mg sodium
6.9 g fat	11 g carbohydrate	254 mg calcium
0.7 g saturated fat	4.6 g sugar	3.6 mg iron
40.8% calories from fat	2.4 g fiber	17.7 mg vitamin C
0 mg cholesterol		1112 mcg beta-carotene
		1 mg vitamin E

ANCHO CHILI

MAKES 10 TO 12 SERVINGS ■ **PREPARATION TIME: 45 minutes** ■ **COOK TIME: 1 hour 30 minutes**

This hearty, flavorful chili will be a hit with your meat-eating friends as well!

4 dried ancho chiles, stemmed and seeded

4 dried pasilla chiles, stemmed and seeded

½ teaspoon cumin seeds

½ teaspoon coriander seeds

1 tablespoon coarsely chopped fresh oregano

2 small onions, chopped

3 garlic cloves, minced

1 (28-ounce) can whole tomatoes, with liquid

¼ cup vegetable broth

1½ cups bulgur wheat

1 cup dried brown lentils

1 (15-ounce) can red kidney beans, drained and rinsed

1. In a large skillet, toast the chiles on each side until browned, about 5 minutes. Remove chiles from skillet and transfer to a bowl. Pour boiling water over chiles and let stand for 30 minutes.
2. Meanwhile, heat skillet over medium-high heat. Add cumin and coriander seeds and toast for 5 minutes until fragrant. Remove seeds to a grinder and grind. Add oregano to the skillet and toast for 3 minutes. Set aside.
3. Reserve one cup of liquid from the chiles and drain the remaining water. Place chiles and reserved liquid in a blender. Add cumin and coriander, oregano, tomatoes and their liquid, onions, and garlic. Purée until smooth.
4. Heat broth in a saucepan over medium heat. Add bulgur wheat and lentils and stir for about 5 minutes. Add chile mixture and 2½ cups water. Bring to a boil. Lower heat and simmer for 30 to 45 minutes, until lentils are tender. Add beans and simmer for 15 minutes.

DID YOU KNOW?

Bulgur wheat is simply a form of whole wheat. It has more fiber and a lower glycemic index compared with refined wheat products.

PER SERVING (¹⁄₁₀ OF RECIPE):

197 calories	10.9 g protein	184 mg sodium
0.8 g fat	39.5 g carbohydrate	65 mg calcium
0.1 g saturated fat	4.1 g sugar	4 mg iron
3.6% calories from fat	10.1 g fiber	9.7 mg vitamin C
0 mg cholesterol		276 mcg beta-carotene
		0.7 mg vitamin E

ASIAN GRILLED TOFU STEAKS *low carb*

MAKES 5 SERVINGS ■ **PREPARATION TIME: 4 hours** ■ **COOK TIME: 15 minutes to cook**

Tofu readily takes up the flavors that are added to it, as you will see with this delicious marinade.

2 (1-pound) blocks extra-firm low-fat tofu

1 cup vegetable broth

3 tablespoons reduced-sodium soy sauce

1 tablespoon hoisin sauce

1 tablespoon dry sherry

1 tablespoon agave nectar

2 garlic cloves, minced

1 tablespoon grated fresh ginger

1 teaspoon orange zest

½ teaspoon arrowroot

Vegetable oil cooking spray

20 wooden skewers, soaked for 1 hour in warm water

¼ cup sliced scallions, for garnish

DID YOU KNOW?

Tofu provides high-quality protein, and has no cholesterol.

1. Wrap blocks of tofu in two layers of paper towels. Place tofu on a plate. Place another plate on top and then place a weight on the top plate (a heavy pan will do). Press for about 1 to 2 hours in the refrigerator.

2. Remove paper towels from tofu and drain all excess water. Pat the tofu dry. Slice tofu into ¾-inch slices.

3. In a medium bowl, mix together broth, soy sauce, hoisin sauce, sherry, agave nectar, garlic, ginger, and orange zest. Whisk well. Arrange tofu in a shallow baking dish. Pour marinade over tofu and marinate, covered, in the refrigerator for 2 hours. Turn tofu slices about halfway through the soaking time.

4. Remove tofu from baking dish and set on a large cutting board. Place marinade in a saucepan and bring to a boil. In a small bowl, combine arrowroot with 2 teaspoons water and mix well. Add to marinade and cook until thickened, about 1 minute. Set aside. Coat an outdoor grill well with cooking spray and set the temperature to high heat.

5. Using two skewers per slice of tofu spaced evenly, slide the skewers through the tofu, with only the tips of the skewers extending through one end of the tofu. The other side should have a good length of skewer for holding onto while turning the tofu on the grill.

6. Place the tofu on the grill and cook on one side for about 4 minutes, basting with some of the reserved marinade. Turn and grill tofu for another 4 minutes, continuing to baste with reserved marinade. Remove tofu to a platter and drizzle with any remaining sauce. Sprinkle with scallions.

PER SERVING (⅕ OF RECIPE):

191 calories	15.6 g protein	563 mg sodium
8.1 g fat	16.5 g carbohydrate	112 mg calcium
1.2 g saturated fat	4.3 g sugar	5.1 mg iron
35.7% calories from fat	5.7 g fiber	3.5 mg vitamin C
0 mg cholesterol		84 mcg beta-carotene
		0.4 mg vitamin E

SWEET AND SOUR TOFU

MAKES 4 SERVINGS ■ PREPARATION TIME: 5 minutes ■ COOK TIME: 25 minutes

This combination of crisp and colorful vegetables, tofu, and a great-tasting sweet and sour sauce is mild and smooth, and appeals to all ages.

FOR THE SAUCE:

⅓ cup pineapple juice

2 tablespoons red wine vinegar

2 tablespoons sugar

1 teaspoon reduced-sodium soy sauce

1 teaspoon grated fresh ginger

2 garlic cloves, minced

2 teaspoons arrowroot

FOR THE TOFU:

½ cup whole wheat pastry flour

1 (1-pound) package extra-firm low-fat tofu, pressed and cut into cubes

¼ cup vegetable broth

1 red bell pepper, thinly sliced

1 green bell pepper, thinly sliced

½ large red onion, thinly sliced

½ cup drained canned pineapple chunks packed in juice

1. Combine all sauce ingredients in a measuring cup and set aside.
2. Pour the flour into a pie pan, and lightly dredge tofu in the flour. Shake off excess flour.
3. Heat the broth in a large skillet or wok over medium-high heat. Sauté tofu until golden brown on both sides, about 2 to 3 minutes.
4. Remove tofu from skillet. Add the bell peppers and onion and stir-fry for 5 minutes. Add the pineapple and sauce and cook until sauce thickens, about 1 minute.

DID YOU KNOW?

Pressing tofu gives it a meaty texture and makes it very receptive to added flavors. To press tofu, just sandwich a tofu block between several layers of paper towels. Place on a plate with another plate on top. Set a weight on top of the plate, and let the tofu drain for 1 to 2 hours. Remove the paper towels, drain, and pat dry. The tofu is now ready to be sliced or cubed.

PER SERVING (¼ OF RECIPE):

229 calories	12.4 g protein	108 mg sodium
5.5 g fat	36.4 g carbohydrate	82 mg calcium
0.8 g saturated fat	16 g sugar	4 mg iron
20% calories from fat	6.5 g fiber	76.5 mg vitamin C
0 mg cholesterol		537 mcg beta-carotene
		0.9 mg vitamin E

SNACKS, DIPS, AND DESSERTS

8

A HEALTHY SNACK keeps you going when it's not quite mealtime. Although many people feel that they shouldn't indulge in snacks, every snack in this book is completely healthy. Made with the best of ingredients, they will reenergize you for the rest of your day.

The difference between a healthful snack and a not-so-good choice is what goes into it. Beef jerky, pork rinds, and mozzarella sticks bring their load of cholesterol and fat, and are missing the healthy complex carbs you need for energy. Ditto for cookies and candy—lots of fat and sugar, and not much nutrition.

But you'll never go wrong with our delicious spreads on crackers or whole-grain bread—they are as healthful as they are delicious. Or keep it simple with fresh fruit. The same considerations apply to desserts. It's all a question of what goes into them. Sometimes the most elegant and fitting desserts are the simplest—slices of fresh fruit, for example. But if your tastes call for something slightly more elaborate, you'll find them here, too.

Instant Snacks

- Cut up some carrots, celery, cantaloupe, or melon, and keep them front and center in the fridge. So when you're hungry and looking for a snack, they are instantly edible, with no preparation required.

- Keep a supply of fruit that travels well, such as apples, firm pears, clementines, or grapes.

- Chickpeas covered in seasoned rice vinegar or low-fat Italian dressing are faster than "fast food," and much healthier! Add chopped celery, peppers, or baby tomatoes for a quick meal, or spoon into pita bread for a great sandwich.

- Make a soy milk and fruit smoothie. Just combine one cup of berries, one cup of soy milk, and four ice cubes. Blend and drink!

CHIPOTLE AND TOMATO SALSA *low carb*

MAKES 4½ CUPS ■ PREPARATION TIME: 25 to 35 minutes

This smoky, spicy salsa is a crowd favorite! Serve with corn tortilla chips.

1 medium onion

1 (28-ounce) can whole peeled tomatoes

3 canned chipotle peppers in adobo sauce, plus 1 tablespoon of adobo sauce

1 teaspoon kosher salt

2 teaspoons lime juice

1. Preheat oven to 350°F.
2. Cut onion into quarters and wrap in foil. Bake until softened, about 20 to 30 minutes.
3. Put onion, tomatoes, peppers and adobo sauce, salt, and lime juice into a food processor. Process until smooth.

DID YOU KNOW?

Chipotles in adobo sauce are a condiment made from chipotles stewed with tomatoes, garlic, vinegar, salt, and spices.

PER 2 TABLESPOONS:

7 calories	0.3 g protein	130 mg sodium
0 g fat	1.8 g carbohydrate	9 mg calcium
0 g saturated fat	1.2 g sugar	0.3 mg iron
5.4% calories from fat	0.3 g fiber	3.8 mg vitamin C
0 mg cholesterol		27 mcg beta-carotene
		0.2 mg vitamin E

FRESH TOMATILLO AND CILANTRO SALSA *low carb*

MAKES 4 1/2 CUPS ■ **PREPARATION TIME: 5 minutes**

This bright, fresh salsa is great with chips, or try it on a baked potato.

1 small sweet onion, chopped

1½ pounds fresh tomatillos, husks removed, chopped

2 jalapeño peppers, stems and seeds removed, chopped

1 cup packed cilantro leaves and tender stems

Juice of 1 lime

1 teaspoon kosher salt

1. Process all ingredients in a food processor until smooth.

DID YOU KNOW?

The tomatillo, or husk tomato, is very popular in Mexican and Guatamalan cuisine and is a close relative of the tomato. It is a staple in Mexican kitchens and serves as the base for a variety of green salsas.

PER SERVING:

7 calories	0.2 g protein	66 mg sodium
0.2 g fat	1.4 g carbohydrate	2 mg calcium
0 g saturated fat	0.6 g sugar	0.1 mg iron
23.3% calories from fat	0.4 g fiber	3 mg vitamin C
0 mg cholesterol		33 mcg beta-carotene
		0.1 mg vitamin E

PICO DE GALLO *low carb*

MAKES 7 CUPS ■ **PREPARATION TIME: 20 minutes**

This salsa is at its best when absolutely fresh. Serve with corn tortilla chips, as a topping for your favorite burrito, or in a cheeseless quesadilla.

1 large sweet onion, such as Maui or Vidalia, chopped

15 Roma tomatoes (about 2 pounds), chopped

2 jalapeño peppers, seeded and chopped

1 cup firmly packed cilantro leaves and tender stems, chopped

1 teaspoon kosher salt

2 tablespoons freshly squeezed lime juice

1. Mix all ingredients together in a large bowl and serve.

DID YOU KNOW?

Literally translated as "rooster's beak," versions of this fresh pico de gallo salsa are sometimes served as a salad in Mexico.

PER 2 TABLESPOONS:

4 calories	0.2 g protein	43 mg sodium
0 g fat	0.9 g carbohydrate	2 mg calcium
0 g saturated fat	0.5 g sugar	0.1 mg iron
7.9% calories from fat	0.2 g fiber	2.4 mg vitamin C
0 mg cholesterol		78 mcg beta-carotene
		0.1 mg vitamin E

low carb

WHITE BEAN AND PIQUILLO PEPPER SPREAD

MAKES 2½ CUPS ■ **PREPARATION TIME: 5 minutes**

The flavors in this robust bean dip will carry you away to Spain. Serve with crackers, pita bread, and fresh vegetables.

2 (15-ounce) cans white beans, drained and rinsed

4 jarred piquillo peppers

1 garlic clove, chopped

1 tablespoon sherry vinegar

1 teaspoon salt

⅛ teaspoon ground black pepper

½ teaspoon smoked paprika

1½ tablespoons Italian parsley leaves

1. Process all ingredients, except parsley, in a food processor until smooth, stopping periodically to scrape down the sides of the bowl. Add parsley and pulse until chopped and just combined.

DID YOU KNOW?

Piquillo peppers are grown in northern Spain and are handpicked, roasted over an open fire, peeled, and packed in their own juices in jars or tins.

PER 2 TABLESPOONS:		
43 calories	2.9 g protein	264 mg sodium
0.1 g fat	7.8 g carbohydrate	28 mg calcium
0 g saturated fat	0.4 g sugar	1.2 mg iron
2.4% calories from fat	2 g fiber	6.3 mg vitamin C
0 mg cholesterol		603 mcg beta-carotene
		0.4 mg vitamin E

CURRIED CHICKPEA SPREAD *low carb*

MAKES 3 CUPS ■ PREPARATION TIME: 25 to 35 minutes

Use your favorite blend of curry powder in this spicy Indian-inspired spread. Serve with crackers, pita bread, and fresh vegetables.

1 medium onion, quartered

3 garlic cloves

2 (15-ounce) cans chickpeas, drained and rinsed

1 tablespoon curry powder

3 tablespoons freshly squeezed lime juice

1¼ teaspoons kosher salt

⅛ teaspoon freshly ground black pepper

1. Preheat the oven to 350°F.
2. Wrap the onion and garlic in aluminum foil. Bake for 20 to 30 minutes, or until softened.
3. Add the onion, garlic, the remaining ingredients, and ¼ cup water to a food processor and process until smooth.

DID YOU KNOW?

Chickpeas, also called garbanzo beans, are one of the world's most widely consumed legumes. Low in fat and a good source of protein, they have gained popularity for their buttery, nutlike taste.

PER 2 TABLESPOONS:

43 calories	2.3 g protein	141 mg sodium
0.7 g fat	7.4 g carbohydrate	15 mg calcium
0.1 g saturated fat	0.4 g sugar	0.8 mg iron
13.1% calories from fat	1.7 g fiber	1.1 mg vitamin C
0 mg cholesterol		6 mcg beta-carotene
		0.1 mg vitamin E

low carb

BISSARA—MIDDLE EASTERN FRESH FAVA BEAN DIP

MAKES ABOUT 3 CUPS ■ **PREPARATION TIME: 45 minutes (5 minutes if using frozen fava beans)**

Fresh fava beans are a spring treat, but your grocery freezer will allow you to enjoy this flavorful dip year round. Serve with pita bread, crostini, vegetables, or crackers.

20 ounces fresh or frozen fava beans, boiled and peeled (see note)

3 tablespoons fresh lemon juice

¾ teaspoon ground cumin

½ cup loosely packed fresh Italian parsley

1 garlic clove

Hot sauce to taste

1 teaspoon salt

Pinch of black pepper

1. Process all ingredients with 2 tablespoons water in a food processor until smooth.

TO PREPARE THE BEANS: Fresh fava beans are commonly sold still in the pod, and the beans must be removed from the pod prior to use. The individual beans are encased in a thick outer membrane called the pericarp, which also must be removed. To prepare the beans for use, bring a large pot of water to a boil. Drop the beans into the boiling water; when the water returns to a boil, drain the beans and rinse under cold water to stop the cooking. The pericarp can now be easily removed with a sharp paring knife. Frozen fava beans may or may not be encased in the pericarp—if the pericarps are present, prepare for use as for the fresh beans. If the beans have already had the membrane removed, drop them into boiling water and cook for about 3 minutes, drain, and rinse under cold water. You will need 20 ounces, or a generous 3 cups, of prepared beans for this recipe.

DID YOU KNOW?

Chinese cooks have used fava beans for at least 5,000 years. They are rich in dietary fiber and folic acid, both of which help prevent cancer.

PER 2 TABLESPOONS:

17 calories	1.3 g protein	125 mg sodium
0.2 g fat	2.9 g carbohydrate	8 mg calcium
0 g saturated fat	0.4 g sugar	0.5 mg iron
7.8% calories from fat	1 g fiber	7.6 mg vitamin C
0 mg cholesterol		126 mcg beta-carotene
		0 mg vitamin E

BASIL PESTO SPREAD *low carb*

MAKES 1½ CUPS ■ PREPARATION TIME: 5 minutes

Try this flavorful spread as a dressing for pasta salad. It can also be served on crackers or as a dip for pita bread or fresh vegetables.

1 cup packed fresh basil leaves

2 garlic cloves, chopped

1 (12.3-ounce) package firm low-fat silken tofu

Kosher salt to taste

Black pepper to taste

1. Place the basil and garlic in a food processor and process until well chopped. Add the tofu and process until smooth. Season with salt and black pepper.

DID YOU KNOW?

Silken tofu has a softer consistency than regular tofu and is used in salad dressings, sauces, and desserts. For best results, drain excess liquid from the tofu and rinse prior to blending or processing. For thicker spreads, start with a fairly dry vegetable or fruit purée and then add the tofu and blend until smooth.

PER 2 TABLESPOONS:

12 calories	1.0 g protein	172 mg sodium
0.3 g fat	0.0 g carbohydrate	16 mg calcium
0 g saturated fat	0.1 g sugar	0.3 mg iron
18.4% calories from fat	0.1 g fiber	0.5 mg vitamin C
0 mg cholesterol		63 mcg beta-carotene
		0 mg vitamin E

SUN-DRIED TOMATO SPREAD *low carb*

MAKES 1¾ CUPS ■ **PREPARATION TIME: 5 minutes**

This spread is excellent with crackers or on a toasted bagel.

½ cup sun-dried tomatoes

2 garlic cloves

1 (12.3-ounce) package firm low-fat silken tofu

¼ cup loosely packed fresh basil leaves

Kosher salt to taste

Black pepper to taste

1. Cover tomatoes in boiling water and allow to soften and re-hydrate for 5 to 10 minutes. Drain and squeeze out any excess water.
2. Place tomatoes in a food processor with garlic and process until well chopped and a paste begins to form. Add tofu, basil, salt, and black pepper and process until smooth.

DID YOU KNOW?

Sun-dried tomato soaking liquid can add flavor to stocks and sauces. Try using wine or vegetable broth instead of water for an even richer flavor.

PER 2 TABLESPOONS:

15 calories	1.9 g protein	209 mg sodium
0.3 g fat	1.6 g carbohydrate	13 mg calcium
0 g saturated fat	0.8 g sugar	0.4 mg iron
15.4% calories from fat	0.3 g fiber	1 mg vitamin C
0 mg cholesterol		24 mcg beta-carotene
		0 mg vitamin E

SPINACH DIP *low carb*

MAKES 2½ CUPS ■ **PREPARATION TIME: 25 to 35 minutes**

This dip is as tasty as it is healthful. If you like, add canned artichokes to make spinach-artichoke dip. Serve it with crackers and pita bread.

1 small onion, quartered

4 garlic cloves

1 (10-ounce) package frozen chopped spinach, thawed

1 (12.3-ounce) package firm low-fat silken tofu

1 tablespoon freshly squeezed lemon juice

1 teaspoon ground coriander

1½ teaspoons kosher salt

¼ teaspoon freshly ground black pepper

Pinch of cayenne pepper

1. Preheat the oven to 350°F.
2. Wrap the onion and garlic in aluminum foil. Bake for 20 to 30 minutes, or until soft.
3. Place the spinach in a clean dish towel. Squeeze and twist the dish towel to press out as much water as possible from the spinach.
4. Place the spinach, onions, and garlic in a food processor and process until well chopped. Add the remaining ingredients and process until smooth.

DID YOU KNOW?

You probably know that spinach is a good source of iron. But did you know that researchers are also looking to see whether green leafy vegetables can protect the eyes against age-related changes? You'll want to be sure to include green leafy vegetables in your daily routine.

PER 2 TABLESPOONS:

12 calories	1.6 g protein	201 mg sodium
0.2 g fat	1.3 g carbohydrate	23 mg calcium
0 g saturated fat	0.3 g sugar	0.4 mg iron
17.6% calories from fat	0.4 g fiber	0.8 mg vitamin C
0 mg cholesterol		680 mcg beta-carotene
		0.4 mg vitamin E

CREAMY FRUIT SMOOTHIE

MAKES 4 SERVINGS ■ PREPARATION TIME: 5 minutes

This is a delicious and refreshing start to the day or a snack to keep you going.

2 cups plain soy, rice, or almond milk

1½ cups fresh blueberries

1 large banana

1 tablespoon flaxseeds

1 tablespoon agave nectar

1. Combine all ingredients in a blender and blend until smooth and flaxseeds are ground. Add ice to the blender if you prefer a frosty cold drink.

DID YOU KNOW?

Bananas hold a good smoothie together. Add any fruit you like: strawberries, mangoes, cherries, blackberries, etc.

PER SERVING (¼ OF RECIPE):

158 calories	5.5 g protein	74 mg sodium
3.4 g fat	29 g carbohydrate	173 mg calcium
0.4 g saturated fat	15.9 g sugar	1.9 mg iron
18.1% calories from fat	4.3 g fiber	8.7 mg vitamin C
0 mg cholesterol		28 mcg beta-carotene
		2.1 mg vitamin E

CHEEZY POPCORN

MAKES 4 SERVINGS ■ **COOK TIME: 5 minutes**

Nutritional yeast adds a cheeselike flavor and keeps the crunch of the popcorn light and flavorful.

½ cup popcorn kernels

1 tablespoon nutritional yeast

1. Pop popcorn kernels in air popper. Transfer the popcorn to large bowl. Sprinkle with nutritional yeast and toss to mix.

DID YOU KNOW?

Red Star nutritional yeast is a delicious source of vitamin B_{12}. It lends a salty, cheesy taste without adding any salt or cheese! Note: Nutritional yeast is not the same as brewer's or baker's yeast, so don't substitute!

PER SERVING (¼ OF RECIPE):

101 calories	4.3 g protein	3 mg sodium
1.2 g fat	19.7 g carbohydrate	3 mg calcium
0.2 g saturated fat	0.2 g sugar	0.9 mg iron
10% calories from fat	4 g fiber	0 mg vitamin C
0 mg cholesterol		21 mcg beta-carotene
		0.1 mg vitamin E

CURRY POPCORN

MAKES 4 SERVINGS ■ **COOK TIME: 5 minutes**

This snack leaves your taste buds popping! Try it, and you'll be hooked.
Snacking should always be this fun.

½ cup popcorn kernels

2 teaspoons curry powder

Vegetable oil cooking
spray

1. Pop popcorn kernels in air popper. Transfer the popcorn to
large bowl. Spray with cooking spray, sprinkle with curry
powder, and mix evenly.

DID YOU KNOW?

What exactly is in curry powder, anyway? It is typically a
blend of coriander, turmeric, cumin, and fenugreek—all
traditional Indian spices. If you don't have premixed
curry powder, you can easily make your own blend.

PER SERVING (¼ OF RECIPE):

96 calories	3.2 g protein	2 mg sodium
1.2 g fat	19.3 g carbohydrate	7 mg calcium
0.2 g saturated fat	0.2 g sugar	1.1 mg iron
10.7% calories from fat	3.8 g fiber	0.1 mg vitamin C
0 mg cholesterol		28 mcg beta-carotene
		0.3 mg vitamin E

FRUIT KABOBS WITH PEACH CREAM DIP

MAKES 6 SERVINGS ■ PREPARATION TIME: 5 minutes

You will love these tasty kabobs. The peach cream flavor is our favorite, but lemon is great, too. For your kabobs, any fruit will do.

1 cup purple seedless grapes

1 cup chopped fresh mango

2 oranges, peeled and chopped

2 bananas, chopped

1 apple, chopped

2 (6-ounce) containers low-fat peach-flavored soy yogurt

1 teaspoon vanilla extract

2 teaspoons ground cinnamon

1. In a small bowl, mix the yogurt, vanilla, and cinnamon.
2. Place six to eight pieces of fruit on each skewer and serve with yogurt dip.

DID YOU KNOW?

Soy yogurt is a healthier alternative to dairy-based yogurt. It provides the same bacterial cultures that serve as healthy probiotics for your digestive system, with no animal fat or cholesterol.

PER SERVING (⅙ OF RECIPE):

161 calories	2.6 g protein	2 mg sodium
1.1 g fat	38.6 g carbohydrate	135 mg calcium
0.2 g saturated fat	28.2 g sugar	0.8 mg iron
5.6% calories from fat	4.6 g fiber	10.0 mg vitamin C
0 mg cholesterol		100 mcg beta-carotene
		0.7 mg vitamin E

CHOCOLATE CHERRY NIRVANA

MAKES 4 SERVINGS ■ **PREPARATION TIME: 5 minutes**

This smoothie is a healthy dessert or snack that can be made in a jiffy. It is best made with frozen cherries to give it that frothy, chilled smoothie taste.

2 cups frozen cherries

2 bananas

1½ cups chocolate soy or rice milk

1. Put all ingredients into a blender and blend until smooth.

DID YOU KNOW?

If your bananas are ripening faster than you can use them, just peel and freeze them for later.

PER SERVING (¼ OF RECIPE):

154 calories	3.4 g protein	49 mg sodium
1.7 g fat	33.8 g carbohydrate	127 mg calcium
0.3 g saturated fat	23.8 g sugar	0.8 mg iron
10% calories from fat	3.4 g fiber	11.6 mg vitamin C
0 mg cholesterol		44 mcg beta-carotene
		0.2 mg vitamin E

ITALIAN CHICKPEA NIBBLES

MAKES 4 SERVINGS ■ **PREPARATION TIME: 5 minutes** ■ **COOK TIME: 10 minutes**

These nibbles are a great snack or appetizer. Toss them into pasta marinara for a hearty sauce.

1 (15-ounce) can chickpeas, drained

1 teaspoon olive oil

½ teaspoon garlic powder

½ teaspoon dried oregano

¼ teaspoon dried basil

¼ teaspoon onion powder

Kosher or sea salt to taste

Freshly ground black pepper to taste

Vegetable oil cooking spray

1. Preheat the oven to 400°F.
2. In a bowl, combine the chickpeas, oil, garlic powder, oregano, basil, onion powder, salt, and black pepper.
3. Coat a baking sheet with cooking spray. Spread the chickpeas onto baking sheet in one layer.
4. Roast the chickpeas until they are nicely browned, about 10 minutes, tossing them halfway through.
5. Remove from the oven and cool chickpeas slightly.

DID YOU KNOW?

Have you ever used chickpeas to make brownies? You'll find oodles of vegan recipes online, made with flour, chocolate chips, chickpeas, egg replacer, and bit of sweetener.

PER SERVING (¼ OF RECIPE):

131 calories	6.5 g protein	323 mg sodium
3 g fat	20.4 g carbohydrate	40 mg calcium
0.4 g saturated fat	0.4 g sugar	2.2 mg iron
19.7% calories from fat	4.6 g fiber	1.2 mg vitamin C
0 mg cholesterol		19 mcg beta-carotene
		0.4 mg vitamin E

RASPBERRY CAKE

MAKES 2 SERVINGS ■ **PREPARATION TIME: 1 hour 15 minutes** ■ **COOK TIME: 30 minutes**

This cake is so easy to make, there's no need to wait for a special occasion to enjoy it!

½ cup all-purpose flour or whole wheat pastry flour

⅛ teaspoon kosher or sea salt

½ teaspoon baking powder

⅛ teaspoon baking soda

3 tablespoons agave nectar

¾ teaspoon apple cider vinegar

½ teaspoon vanilla extract

5 tablespoons soy milk

3 tablespoons Grand Marnier

½ cup plus 3 tablespoons fresh raspberries

1 teaspoon slivered almonds, for garnish

1. Preheat the oven to 350°F.
2. In a medium bowl, whisk the flour, salt, baking powder, and baking soda. In a separate small bowl, whisk the agave nectar, vinegar, vanilla, and soy milk. Add the wet ingredients to dry ingredients and stir to combine.
3. Pour batter into a 4-inch mini-cake pan or springform pan. Bake for 30 minutes, or until a toothpick inserted in the center comes out clean. Cool on a rack for about 10 minutes, and then carefully remove from the pan.
4. Pour Grand Marnier over the cake and let sit for at least 1 hour.
5. Place ½ cup raspberries in a small saucepan and cook over medium-low heat. As they soften, press them with a spoon to break them up and release their juices. Once raspberries are completely soft and there is liquid on the bottom of the pan, transfer them to a blender and purée. Press the purée through a fine-mesh strainer to remove seeds.
6. Pour the sauce over the top of the cake and garnish with the remaining 3 tablespoons raspberries and the almonds. Serve immediately.

DID YOU KNOW?

Raspberries come in a variety of colors, including several shades of red, purple, black, and even yellow!

PER SERVING (½ OF CAKE):

319 calories	5.3 g protein	383 mg sodium
1.8 g fat	63.1 g carbohydrate	198 mg calcium
0.2 g saturated fat	26.3 g sugar	3.8 mg iron
4.7% calories from fat	4.3 g fiber	11.2 mg vitamin C
0 mg cholesterol		5 mcg beta-carotene
		1.2 mg vitamin E

CREAMY WHITE BEAN AND ARTICHOKE DIP *low carb*

MAKES 2 CUPS ■ PREPARATION TIME: 10 minutes ■ COOK TIME: 35 minutes

This flavorful dip is bright with herbs and zesty garlic. Serve with whole wheat pita bread triangles or crudités.

1 small white onion, chopped

1 (15-ounce) can artichoke hearts, drained

1 or 2 small garlic cloves, passed through a garlic press

1 (15-ounce) can white beans, drained and rinsed

1 tablespoon lemon juice

1 tablespoon finely chopped scallions

1 teaspoon fresh oregano

1 tablespoon chopped fresh basil

Pinch of cayenne pepper

Sea salt to taste

Black pepper to taste

1. Preheat the oven to 425°F.
2. Wrap the onion in foil and bake for 20 minutes.
3. Squeeze each of the artichoke hearts or press them against the bottom of a fine-mesh colander with a spoon to force out as much moisture as possible.
4. Add the onions, artichoke hearts, and all remaining ingredients to a blender or food processor and purée until smooth, but still chunky.

DID YOU KNOW?

Artichokes are high in fiber, folate, and potassium, and supply a surprising amount of vitamin C, as well. When puréed, their texture mimics cream.

PER 2 TABLESPOONS:

38 calories	2.4 g protein	223 mg sodium
0.2 g fat	7.4 g carbohydrate	24 mg calcium
0 g saturated fat	0.5 g sugar	0.9 mg iron
3.4% calories from fat	2.8 g fiber	2 mg vitamin C
0 mg cholesterol		15 mcg beta-carotene
		0.2 mg vitamin E

BAKED APPLES IN PHYLLO DOUGH

MAKES 6 SERVINGS ■ **PREPARATION TIME: 15 minutes** ■ **COOK TIME: 30 minutes**

Reminiscent of apple strudel, these phyllo packets make for a light dessert or a great sweet snack.

2 Jonathan or Rome apples

1 teaspoon ground cinnamon

¼ teaspoon ground allspice

¼ teaspooon ground cardamom

2 tablespoons agave nectar

2 tablespoons raisins

12 to 15 sheets phyllo dough

1. Preheat the oven to 350°F. Core and thinly slice each apple. Place the apple slices in a bowl.

2. In a separate small bowl, mix the cinnamon, allspice, and cardamom together. Add the agave nectar and mix to form a loose paste. Pour this mixture over the apples and stir to coat well. Stir in the raisins.

3. Place two sheets of phyllo atop each other. Spoon one-sixth of the apple mixture into the center of the phyllo sheet. Fold the top and bottom edges of the phyllo over the apples. Repeat with the two sides, forming a rectangular packet. Place this packet seam side down in a large glass baking dish. Repeat with the remaining apples and phyllo for a total of six packets.

4. Bake for about 30 minutes. Can be served warm or at room temperature.

DID YOU KNOW?

The wonderful earthy taste of this recipe comes from cardamom. By weight, it is one of the most expensive spices in the world—only saffron and vanilla are more expensive. Luckily, you only need ¼ teaspoon!

PER SERVING (⅙ OF RECIPE):

185 calories	3.5 g protein	149 mg sodium
0.5 g fat	42 g carbohydrate	29 mg calcium
0.1 g saturated fat	10.4 g sugar	2 mg iron
2.4% calories from fat	2.6 g fiber	2.2 mg vitamin C
0 mg cholesterol		13 mcg beta-carotene
		0.1 mg vitamin E

9

ENTERTAINING

THESE ENTERTAINING MENUS are a delight for the senses. Whether you choose an Italian feast, trendy tapas, a summertime sensibility, or an Asian-style dinner, your guests will be impressed by your creativity and thoughtfulness.

When we dine with others, we do more than share a meal. The foods we serve communicate what we think of ourselves, and what we think of our guests. These intriguing menus will delight your guests with wonderful flavors and a real sense of healthfulness. They will also spark endless conversations; there is no more popular topic than food and health. With these wonderful menus, you're not just a great host; you're the expert.

Often it can seem daunting to stick to a special diet on special occasions—let alone serve one. As every experienced host knows, so many guests these days are trying to eat more healthfully than people did a generation ago. And many guests feel they are walking a tightrope between their desire to stick to their healthful resolve and their desire to show appreciation to their hosts who have cooked up all manner of artery-clogging treats.

Well, now there are easy, healthful, and delicious entertaining choices that let you take a bow for offering an event that is delicious and healthful. We present four complete menus for you here, and they will undoubtedly inspire many other variations.

ENTERTAINING MENU #1:
Italian Feast

THIS GREAT MENU takes advantage of summer's great fruits and vegetables. You can roast the beets and make the dressing the day before your dinner party. Just keep them in the refrigerator until you are ready to assemble the salad. You can even dice all of your vegetables for the pasta and peppers well before serving. You'll need about 30 to 45 minutes to pull the meal together. Bring your guests out onto the back deck and serve this menu al fresco (and let them grill the peaches!). Keep an eye on that balsamic glaze—it's so tasty it might just disappear before dessert!

SPINACH, BEET, AND ORANGE SALAD WITH GINGER-AGAVE DRESSING

MAKES 4 SERVINGS ■ **PREPARATION TIME: 20 minutes** ■ **COOK TIME: 1 hour and 20 minutes**

Beets pair beautifully with citrus, and this salad is a delicious example. Beets come in a variety of colors—not only several shades of red and purple, but also pink, yellow, and even white!

FOR THE DRESSING:

4 tablespoons rice vinegar

2 tablespoons agave nectar

2 teaspoons paprika

2 teaspoons grated fresh ginger

½ teaspoon chili powder

Juice of 1 lime

FOR THE SALAD:

2 small beets, scrubbed and trimmed, stems removed

6 cups baby spinach

2 medium oranges, peeled and cut into sections

1. To prepare the dressing: Put the vinegar, agave nectar, paprika, ginger, and chili powder into a saucepan and bring to a boil. Add lime juice. Let dressing cool.

2. Preheat the oven to 400°F. Seal each beet in foil and place them on a baking sheet. Roast the beets until fork tender; this may take as little as 40 minutes or as much as 1 hour and 20 minutes, depending on the size of the beets. Let the beets cool, unwrap, and peel them under running water. Cut them into bite-size wedges.

3. Arrange spinach on a platter and top with beets and oranges. Drizzle dressing over the spinach salad.

DID YOU KNOW?

Have you ever wondered what to do with those beautiful green leafy beet tops? They are very nutritious and can be lightly steamed or served fresh in a salad mix.

PER SERVING (¼ OF RECIPE):

89 calories	2.5 g protein	59 mg sodium
0.5 g fat	20.6 g carbohydrate	100 mg calcium
0.1 g saturated fat	13.5 g sugar	2.3 mg iron
5% calories from fat	3.5 g fiber	51.1 mg vitamin C
0 mg cholesterol		2947 mcg beta-carotene
		1.5 mg vitamin E

WHOLE WHEAT PASTA with ZUCCHINI and HERBS

MAKES FOUR 2-CUP SERVINGS ■ **PREPARATION TIME: 40 minutes** ■ **COOK TIME: 25 minutes**

This bright and colorful pasta takes advantage of the best of summer's produce and herbs.

¼ cup vegetable broth

½ cup chopped onion

2 garlic cloves, thinly sliced

2 pounds fresh plum tomatoes, peeled, seeded, and chopped

1 (16-ounce) package dry whole wheat penne pasta

1½ cups zucchini, chopped into ¼-inch cubes

¼ cup finely chopped fresh basil

1 tablespoon finely chopped fresh oregano

Kosher or sea salt to taste

Freshly ground black pepper to taste

1. Heat the broth in a large skillet over medium heat. Add the onion and garlic and sauté for about 5 to 6 minutes. Add the tomatoes and any accumulated tomato juice and increase heat to medium-high. Cook for about 15 minutes until the liquid evaporates. Note: If tomatoes dry out before the end of this cooking period, add ¼ to ½ cup water to keep them from scorching.
2. Meanwhile, bring about 6 quarts of water to a boil. Add a pinch of salt to the water. Put in the pasta and cook for about 8 to 9 minutes. Add the zucchini and cook for 2 minutes. Drain the pasta and zucchini, reserving about ½ cup cooking water.
3. Mix the pasta with the tomato sauce, along with ½ cup cooking water. Add the basil, oregano, salt, and black pepper and toss well.

DID YOU KNOW?

Oregano is a staple in Italian cuisine, but don't confuse it with Mexican oregano, which is similar in flavor but more closely related to lemon verbena.

PER SERVING (¼ OF RECIPE):

337 calories	14.7 g protein	270 mg sodium
1.5 g fat	72.8 g carbohydrate	74 mg calcium
0.3 g saturated fat	7.4 g sugar	4 mg iron
3.8% calories from fat	8.7 g fiber	40.5 mg vitamin C
0 mg cholesterol		849 mcg beta-carotene
		1.6 mg vitamin E

MULTICOLORED PEPPERS WITH THYME *low carb*

MAKES 4 SERVINGS ■ **PREPARATION TIME: 5 minutes** ■ **COOK TIME: 10 minutes**

This dish is tasty, colorful, and very flexible. Substitute any fresh herbs you have for the thyme.

½ cup vegetable broth

1 red bell pepper, cut into ¼-inch strips

1 yellow bell pepper, cut into ¼-inch strips

1 orange bell pepper, cut into ¼-inch strips

1 green bell pepper, cut into ¼-inch strips

2 teaspoons minced fresh thyme

Kosher or sea salt to taste

Freshly ground black pepper to taste

1. Heat the broth in a large skillet over medium-high heat. Add the bell peppers and sauté for 10 minutes, until peppers are soft. Sprinkle with fresh thyme, salt, and black pepper.

DID YOU KNOW?

Bell peppers have a recessive gene that prevents the formation of capsaicin, the chemical compound that makes other peppers spicy.

PER SERVING (¼ OF RECIPE):

34 calories	1.2 g protein	267 mg sodium
0.3 g fat	8.1 g carbohydrate	15 mg calcium
0 g saturated fat	6.2 g sugar	0.6 mg iron
6.2% calories from fat	1.3 g fiber	157.8 mg vitamin C
0 mg cholesterol		623 mcg beta-carotene
		0.8 mg vitamin E

GRILLED PEACHES with SWEET BALSAMIC GLAZE

MAKES 4 SERVINGS ■ PREPARATION TIME: 5 minutes ■ COOK TIME: 30 minutes

In this delightful recipe, two techniques—grilling and reduction—bring out the best of each ingredient, creating a dessert that is bursting with flavor. When grilled, peaches become almost caramelized, creating a sensationally sweet flavor without added sugars. Boiling balsamic vinegar and reducing it by half transforms it into a smooth flavorful syrup. Made with simple ingredients, this dessert is a spectacular finish to any meal.

4 ripe peaches, halved and pitted

Butter-flavor vegetable oil cooking spray

½ cup good quality balsamic vinegar

1 tablespoon brown sugar

1 tablespoon lemon juice

1 teaspoon almond extract

Fresh mint sprigs

1. Heat a gas grill to medium-high. Coat peach halves with cooking spray (use about two sprays per peach half).
2. Place peaches cut side down on the grill and grill for about 4 to 5 minutes per side until grill marks appear and peaches are slightly softened.
3. While peaches are grilling, prepare the glaze. Add vinegar to a small saucepan over medium-high heat. Boil vinegar until it is reduced by half and looks thick. Add sugar, lemon juice, and almond extract.
4. Remove peaches from the grill and place cut side up on a dessert dish. Drizzle with balsamic glaze and garnish with a mint sprig.

DID YOU KNOW?

Peaches are loaded with potassium, which helps lower blood pressure.

PER SERVING (⅛ OF RECIPE):

88 calories	1 g protein	15 mg sodium
0.1 g fat	20.1 g carbohydrate	16 mg calcium
0 g saturated fat	16.6 g sugar	0.9 mg iron
1.2% calories from fat	2.6 g fiber	6.7 mg vitamin C
0 mg cholesterol		524 mcg beta-carotene
		1 mg vitamin E

ENTERTAINING MENU #2:
Tapas

THE HOME OF small plates, Spanish cuisine offers wonderful flavors in every bite. This tapas menu provides a variety of textures, from a crispy Roasted Pepper Bruschetta to tender Chickpeas with Onion and Tomatoes. You might want to prepare the Eggplant Salad a day before—its flavors blossom as it chills in the refrigerator. But be careful: You'll want to decrease the amount of garlic if you're making the salad ahead of time since the garlic flavor will get stronger. Don't forget to pick up some nice crusty bread to accompany this feast.

ROASTED PEPPER BRUSCHETTA

MAKES SIX 2-SLICE SERVINGS ■ PREPARATION TIME: 5 minutes ■ COOK TIME: 45 minutes

2 red bell peppers

2 yellow bell peppers

2 tablespoons finely chopped fresh basil

2 tablespoons balsamic vinegar

1 Italian baguette (preferably whole wheat), cut into 12 slices

3 large garlic cloves, peeled and cut in half

Salt to taste

Black pepper to taste

VARIATION: To put an another spin on this recipe, substitute balsamic syrup for balsamic vinegar. Here is how you make it: Place ½ cup balsamic vinegar and 1 teaspoon agave nectar in a small saucepan. Boil vinegar until it is reduced by half the original amount. Boiled-down balsamic vinegar has a wonderful rich flavor, is less acidic on your palate, and has a more refined taste.

1. To prepare the roasted peppers, place bell peppers whole directly into the flame of a gas burner. With long-handled tongs, turn peppers until skins have blackened (don't worry that every inch is blackened, a little red or yellow skin is okay). Place peppers in a bowl, cover with plastic wrap, and let cool. Alternatively, if you do not have a gas stove, halve bell peppers and remove membranes and seeds. Place pepper halves onto a broiler tray or baking sheet, cut side down. Broil about 4 inches from the heat source until blackened. Proceed as directed above.

2. Preheat the oven to 400°F.

3. When peppers have cooled, drain any of the remaining juices and remove blackened skin with your fingertips or use a paper towel. Do not rinse under water. Do not worry if some blackened skin remains on the peppers, it is actually delicious! Slice peppers into ¼-inch strips. Toss peppers in a bowl with basil and balsamic vinegar. Season with salt and black pepper.

4. Place bread slices on a baking sheet. Toast bread in the oven for about 2 to 3 minutes on each side until toasted but the bread has not turned brown. Remove bread from the oven and immediately rub each slice with garlic (just the top side is enough). Distribute the roasted pepper mixture on top of the bread and serve.

PER 2-SLICE SERVING:		
185 calories	7.3 g protein	502 mg sodium
1.2 g fat	37.2 g carbohydrate	39 mg calcium
0.3 g saturated fat	9.5 g sugar	2.5 mg iron
5.6% calories from fat	2.2 g fiber	124 mg vitamin C
0 mg cholesterol		655 mcg beta-carotene
		0.9 mg vitamin E

GARLIC MUSHROOMS *low carb*

MAKES SIX ½-CUP SERVINGS ■ PREPARATION TIME: 10 minutes ■ COOK TIME: 15 minutes

1 cup vegetable broth

2 (8-ounce) containers mushrooms, quartered

4 garlic cloves, thinly sliced

1 teaspoon smoked paprika

¼ teaspoon crushed red pepper

2 tablespoon dry sherry or sherry vinegar

Kosher or sea salt to taste

Black pepper to taste

½ cup finely chopped fresh parsley

1. Heat ¼ cup broth a large skillet over medium heat. Put in the mushrooms and cook for 2 minutes without stirring. Stir and cook for about 5 minutes, until mushrooms begin to brown. Add the garlic, paprika, and red pepper. Cook for 2 minutes.

2. Add the sherry and cook until it evaporates. Add the remaining ¾ cup broth and season with salt and black pepper. Bring to a boil, lower heat, and simmer for 3 minutes. Pour the mixture into a bowl and sprinkle with parsley.

PER SERVING (⅙ OF RECIPE):		
30 calories	1.5 g protein	309 mg sodium
0.4 g fat	5.1 g carbohydrate	16 mg calcium
0 g saturated fat	0.8 g sugar	1.4 mg iron
9.7% calories from fat	1.5 g fiber	9.6 mg vitamin C
0 mg cholesterol		409 mcg beta-carotene
		0.2 mg vitamin E

CHICKPEAS WITH ONION AND TOMATO *low carb*

MAKES SIX ½-CUP SERVINGS ■ PREPARATION TIME: 10 minutes ■ COOK TIME: 25 minutes

¼ cup vegetable broth

1 medium onion, chopped

3 plum tomatoes, peeled, seeded, and chopped

2 garlic cloves, minced

1 bay leaf

½ teaspoon dried oregano

1 (15-ounce) can chickpeas, drained and rinsed

Kosher or sea salt to taste

Freshly ground black pepper to taste

1. Heat the broth in a skillet over medium-high heat. Add onion and cook for 5 minutes. Put in the tomatoes and garlic and cook for 3 minutes. Add the bay leaf and oregano. Lower heat, cover, and set heat to a low simmer for about 10 to 15 minutes.

2. Put in the chickpeas, salt, and black pepper and cook for an additional 5 minutes, or until chickpeas are heated through.

PER SERVING (⅙ OF RECIPE):

92 calories	4.8 g protein	225 mg sodium
1.3 g fat	16.2 g carbohydrate	33 mg calcium
0.1 g saturated fat	1.6 g sugar	1.7 mg iron
12% calories from fat	3.4 g fiber	6.6 mg vitamin C
0 mg cholesterol		83 mcg beta-carotene
		0.3 mg vitamin E

EGGPLANT SALAD *low carb*

MAKES 6 SERVINGS ■ PREPARATION TIME: 10 minutes ■ COOK TIME: 50 minutes

1 pound eggplant

2 red bell peppers

2 tomatoes, seeded and chopped

2 garlic cloves, minced

¼ cup finely chopped red onion

¼ cup chopped fresh parsley

2 teaspoons red wine vinegar

2 teaspoons Dijon mustard

Pinch of sugar

Kosher or sea salt to taste

Freshly ground black pepper to taste

1. Preheat the oven to 400°F. Remove the stem from the eggplant and cut the eggplant in half. Cut the bell peppers in half and remove the seeds and membrane. Place the eggplant and peppers on a baking sheet covered with parchment paper and roast for about 25 to 30 minutes until soft. Place the peppers in a bowl and cover with plastic wrap, until cool enough to handle.

2. Peel the skin off the peppers and cut into strips. Scoop out the flesh of the eggplant and mash, then drain any extra liquid.

3. Place the peppers and eggplant in a large bowl. Add the tomatoes, garlic, onion, and parsley. In a small bowl, mix together the vinegar, mustard, sugar, salt, and black pepper. Pour the dressing onto the salad and mix well. Cover and refrigerate for at least 1 hour prior to serving.

PER SERVING (⅙ OF RECIPE):		
46 calories	1.5 g protein	194 mg sodium
0.4 g fat	10.6 g carbohydrate	20 mg calcium
0.1 g saturated fat	6.3 g sugar	0.7 mg iron
7.9% calories from fat	2.7 g fiber	75.2 mg vitamin C
0 mg cholesterol		911 mcg beta-carotene
		1.1 mg vitamin E

ENTERTAINING MENU #3:
Summertime Party

THIS MENU CAPTURES the best of Italy and summertime. If you have a farmers' market in your area, buy local asparagus and strawberries in season—you won't believe how fresh and flavorful they are! You can start this menu ahead of time by marinating the mushrooms and macerating the strawberries. You can even prepare the salad in advance; just wait to toss the salad with vinaigrette until just before serving. Allow yourself about an hour to cook the risotto, grill the mushrooms, and finish the meal. And be sure to invite your guests into the kitchen to help stir the risotto—give everyone a turn with the spoon!

GRILLED PORTOBELLO MUSHROOMS *low carb*

MAKES 6 GRILLED MUSHROOMS ■ **PREPARATION TIME:** 10 minutes plus 1 to 2 hours for marinating the mushrooms ■ **COOK TIME:** 5 to 10 minutes

6 medium portobello mushrooms

6 garlic cloves, sliced

6 tablespoons lemon juice

6 tablespoons balsamic vinegar

3 tablespoons chopped fresh basil

1 tablespoon minced garlic

Kosher salt to taste

Freshly ground black pepper to taste

Vegetable oil cooking spray

1. Remove stems from mushrooms and discard. Wipe mushroom caps with a paper towel to remove any surface dirt.
2. Tuck garlic slices into the gills of the mushrooms. Space out the garlic slices so the entire mushroom has garlic divided throughout.
3. Place mushrooms in a large baking pan. Mix together the lemon juice, vinegar, basil, minced garlic, salt, and black pepper. Pour over the mushrooms and let marinate for 1 to 2 hours.
4. Remove the mushrooms from the marinade. Coat a grill rack with cooking spray. Grill the mushrooms over medium-high heat, turning once, about 2 to 3 minutes per side, basting with any leftover marinade.

DID YOU KNOW?

To store mushrooms, place them in a brown paper bag and onto a refrigerator shelf rather than in the crisper, to avoid excess humidity. They will keep for 2 to 3 days.

PER GRILLED MUSHROOM:

44 calories	2.8 g protein	161 mg sodium
0.5 g fat	8 g carbohydrate	19 mg calcium
0 g saturated fat	2.8 g sugar	0.6 mg iron
9.4% calories from fat	1.4 g fiber	5.4 mg vitamin C
0 mg cholesterol		42 mcg beta-carotene
		0 mg vitamin E

SAFFRON RISOTTO WITH PEAS AND ASPARAGUS

MAKES 6 SERVINGS ■ PREPARATION TIME: 15 to 20 minutes ■ COOK TIME: 30 minutes

8½ cups vegetable broth

1 large onion, chopped

1 large leek, white part only, thinly sliced

3 garlic cloves, minced

2½ cups Arborio rice

Kosher or sea salt to taste

Freshly ground black pepper to taste

Large pinch of saffron threads

½ cup dry white wine

½ pound asparagus, trimmed and cut into 2-inch lengths

1 cup frozen green peas

½ cup chopped fresh basil

1. In a large skillet or saucepan, heat ½ cup broth over medium heat. Add the onion, leek, and garlic and sauté for 3 minutes. Add the rice and sauté for 5 minutes; keep stirring the rice as you sauté to keep it from sticking to the bottom of the pan. Season with salt and black pepper.

2. In a separate pot, heat 8 cups broth. Crumble in the saffron threads and stir to dissolve. Not all threads will dissolve and this is okay. Add the wine to the rice and cook until the rice absorbs the liquid.

3. Add a ladleful of broth to the rice and stir again until the liquid is absorbed. Stir in the asparagus, peas, and basil. Keep adding broth a ladleful at a time to the rice until all the broth is gone and the rice is creamy. This entire process takes about 20 to 25 minutes.

DID YOU KNOW?

Saffron is made from the dried stigmas of the saffron crocus flower. It takes a football-sized field of flowers—about 50,000 to 75,000 flowers—to make a pound of dried saffron.

PER SERVING (⅙ OF RECIPE):

375 calories	8.5 g protein	1502 mg sodium
0.9 g fat	78.6 g carbohydrate	59 mg calcium
0.2 g saturated fat	6.4 g sugar	3.7 mg iron
1.9% calories from fat	2.4 g fiber	6.4 mg vitamin C
0 mg cholesterol		834 mcg beta-carotene
		0.5 mg vitamin E

FENNEL AND TOMATO SALAD WITH FENNEL VINAIGRETTE *low carb*

MAKES 6 SERVINGS ■ PREPARATION TIME: 15 minutes

2 tablespoons white wine vinegar

2 teaspoons Dijon mustard

1 garlic clove, minced

1 teaspoon fennel seeds, ground in a coffee or spice grinder

2 large red or yellow tomatoes, sliced in half and cut into thin wedges

2 medium fennel bulbs, trimmed and julienned into ¼-inch pieces

¼ cup thinly sliced red onion

6 cups mixed greens

1. In a small bowl, whisk the vinegar, mustard, garlic, and ground fennel seeds.
2. In a salad bowl, combine the tomatoes, fresh fennel, onion, and greens. Add the dressing and toss lightly to coat.

DID YOU KNOW?

Fennel's aromatic taste is similar to licorice and anise. In fact, it is often mistakenly referred to as anise in the marketplace.

PER SERVING (⅙ OF RECIPE):

51 calories	2.5 g protein	102 mg sodium
0.6 g fat	10.7 g carbohydrate	78 mg calcium
0.1 g saturated fat	3.7 g sugar	1.5 mg iron
9.3% calories from fat	4.5 g fiber	26.5 mg vitamin C
0 mg cholesterol		2010 mcg beta-carotene
		0.8 mg vitamin E

STRAWBERRIES IN MARSALA *low carb*

MAKES SIX ½-CUP SERVINGS ■ **PREPARATION TIME: 5 minutes + 1 hour to macerate**

3 cups hulled and quartered strawberries

1 tablespoon light agave nectar

2 tablespoons Marsala wine

1. Combine all ingredients and let macerate for 1 hour. Serve in dessert cups.

DID YOU KNOW?

Marsala is a fortified wine produced in the region surrounding Marsala, Sicily.

PER SERVING (⅙ OF RECIPE):		
45 calories	0.6 g protein	3 mg sodium
0.3 g fat	9.7 g carbohydrate	21 mg calcium
0 g saturated fat	6.4 g sugar	0.5 mg iron
4.7% calories from fat	1.7 g fiber	48.8 mg vitamin C
0 mg cholesterol		6 mcg beta-carotene
		0.2 mg vitamin E

ENTERTAINING MENU #4:
Asian Twist

THIS MENU EXPLORES the flavors of Asian cooking—
and is virtually foolproof! Although easy to prepare,
plan for an hour to complete this menu. To help with
the timing, begin with the soup (this can stay heated on
the stove) and prepare the salad while the tofu and lo
mein are marinating. And don't forget the chopsticks!

LEMONGRASS AND MUSHROOM SOUP *low carb*

MAKES 4 SERVINGS ■ **PREPARATION TIME: 10 minutes** ■ **COOK TIME: 30 minutes**

4½ cups vegetable broth

1 large shallot, finely chopped

2 garlic cloves, thinly sliced

1 lemongrass stalk, bottom part only, finely chopped

1 medium carrot, thinly sliced

2 cups shiitake mushrooms, stems removed, thinly sliced

2 tablespoons reduced-sodium soy sauce

1 tablespoon dry sherry

¼ to ½ teaspoon chili purée (also called chili sauce and can be found in the Asian section of your market)

1. In a large saucepan, heat ½ cup broth over medium heat. Add the shallot, garlic, and lemongrass and sauté for 2 minutes. Add the carrot and mushrooms and sauté for 3 minutes.

2. Add the remaining 4 cups broth and bring to a boil. Lower the heat and simmer for 20 minutes. In a small bowl, combine the soy sauce, sherry, and chili purée. Add to the soup and simmer for 3 more minutes.

PER SERVING (¼ OF RECIPE):		
47 calories	1.2 g protein	1338 mg sodium
0.1 g fat	10.4 g carbohydrate	21 mg calcium
0 g saturated fat	4.3 g sugar	0.6 mg iron
2.1% calories from fat	1.2 g fiber	3.7 mg vitamin C
0 mg cholesterol		1480 mcg beta-carotene
		0.2 mg vitamin E

MIXED GREENS with MISO DRESSING *low carb*

MAKES 4 SERVINGS ■ PREPARATION TIME: 15 minutes

FOR THE DRESSING:

¼ cup yellow miso

3 tablespoons whole-grain mustard

2 tablespoon apple cider vinegar

1 tablespoon rice vinegar

Sea salt to taste

Freshly ground black pepper to taste

FOR THE SALAD:

4 cups mixed salad greens

2 carrots, shredded

1 cup shredded red cabbage

½ cup thinly sliced cucumber

1. Whisk dressing ingredients with 3 tablespoons water in a small bowl and set aside.
2. Place the salad greens on a platter, then spread the carrots, cabbage, and cucumber over the greens. Drizzle with dressing and serve.

DID YOU KNOW?

Miso is a rich, salty condiment that characterizes the essence of Japanese cooking. Traditional miso is made from fermented soybeans. Variations in length of aging produce many types that differ greatly in flavor, texture, color, and aroma. A Japanese breakfast often begins with a fortifying bowl of miso soup, and miso flavors a variety of other foods throughout the day. You'll find miso in the refrigerated section of natural food stores and in Asian markets.

PER SERVING (¼ OF RECIPE):

74 calories	4 g protein	963 mg sodium
1.8 g fat	11.8 g carbohydrate	65 mg calcium
0.3 g saturated fat	4.4 g sugar	1.6 mg iron
19.8% calories from fat	3.8 g fiber	21.1 mg vitamin C
0 mg cholesterol		4329 mcg beta-carotene
		0.7 mg vitamin E

VEGETABLE LO MEIN

MAKES 4 SERVINGS ■ PREPARATION TIME: 20 minutes ■ COOK TIME: 15 minutes

1 (8-ounce) package udon noodles

3 tablespoons reduced-sodium soy sauce

1 tablespoon rice vinegar

1 tablespoon plus 2 teaspoons arrowroot

8 ounces extra-firm tofu, (half of a package) pressed and cut into 1-inch cubes

1 cup vegetable broth

3 tablespoons hoisin sauce

½ teaspoon chili purée with garlic

Vegetable oil cooking spray

1 tablespoon grated fresh ginger

3 garlic cloves, minced

1 red bell pepper, thinly sliced

2 celery stalks, thinly sliced on a diagonal

1 cup broccoli florets

1 cup sugar snap peas

1. Cook the udon noodles according to package directions. Drain and set aside.
2. In a large bowl, combine 2 tablespoons soy sauce, vinegar, and 2 teaspoons arrowroot. Mix well, add the tofu and mix gently. Let stand for 15 minutes.
3. In a measuring cup, mix together the remaining 1 tablespoon soy sauce, 1 tablespoon arrowroot, ½ cup broth, hoisin sauce, and chili purée. Mix well and set aside
4. Spray a large wok (or large skillet) with cooking spray. Add the tofu with its marinade to wok and stir-fry tofu until browned on all sides. Remove tofu and set aside.
5. Heat ¼ cup broth in the wok. Add the ginger and garlic and stir-fry for 30 seconds. Add the bell pepper, celery, and broccoli. Stir-fry for 1 minute. Pour in the remaining ¼ cup broth, cover, and steam vegetables for 2 to 3 minutes. Put in the sugar snap peas, cover, and steam for 1 to 2 minutes. Add the tofu and stir-fry for 1 minute. Pour in the sauce and turn to coat the tofu and vegetables. Put in the cooked udon noodles and turn to cover the noodles with sauce.

PER SERVING (¼ OF RECIPE):		
314 calories	16.1 g protein	873 mg sodium
4.8 g fat	56.8 g carbohydrate	160 mg calcium
0.6 g saturated fat	6.2 g sugar	3.7 mg iron
12.8% calories from fat	6.8 g fiber	72.3 mg vitamin C
0 mg cholesterol		850 mcg beta-carotene
		1.5 mg vitamin E

FRESH STRAWBERRY PIE

MAKES 8 SERVINGS ■ **PREPARATION TIME: 20 minutes + 2 hours to set**

1⅓ cups pitted dates

1½ tablespoons orange juice

2 cups coarsely crushed graham cracker crumbs

2 tablespoons agave nectar

1½ cups whole strawberries, hulled

¼ teaspoon ground cardamom

2 cups sliced strawberries

BANANA CASHEW CREAM (OPTIONAL):

¼ banana

¼ cup raw cashews, soaked for at least 6 hours

1. Purée the dates and orange juice in a food processor or blender. Separate one-quarter of the purée to use in the strawberry filling.
2. Mash the date purée and graham cracker crumbs together with your hands to fully combine them. Pat the crust into a glass pie dish.
3. Stir together the agave nectar, whole strawberries, and cardamom. Add the remaining date pureé and sliced strawberries. Spread the mixture in the pie dish and refrigerate for 2 hours.
4. Make sure that the pie has completely set, otherwise it will fall apart as you slice it. If using, top each slice with a dollop of Banana Cashew Cream.
5. To make the Banana Cashew Cream: Blend the banana and cashews with 2 tablespoons water in a food processor or blender until creamy. Refrigerate until ready to use.

DID YOU KNOW?

Strawberries are thought to have been first cultivated in ancient Rome, and the plant is part of the rose family.

PER SERVING (⅛ OF PIE):

196 calories	2.7 g protein	132 mg sodium
2.3 g fat	44.2 g carbohydrate	50 mg calcium
0.4 g saturated fat	27.5 g sugar	1.5 mg iron
10.4% calories from fat	4.2 g fiber	41.5 mg vitamin C
0 mg cholesterol		7 mcg beta-carotene
		0.4 mg vitamin E

A THREE-DAY
MENU PLAN

DAY ONE

▶ 1 serving Spanish-Style Scrambler Wrap (page 59)

▶ ½ cup fresh blueberries

▶ 1 serving Cauliflower and Sweet Potato Chowder (page 74)

▶ 1 cup fresh spinach tossed with sliced red onion, ½ cup sliced carrots, ¼ cup diced strawberries sprinkled with lemon juice

▶ 1 small whole-grain roll

▶ 1 serving Chipotle and Tomato Salsa (page 155)

▶ 1 ounce fat-free baked tortilla chips

▶ Soba Noodles with Chinese Vegetables (page 110)

▶ Steamed fresh asparagus, squeeze of lemon

▶ ½ cup vanilla soy yogurt mixed with ½ sliced banana

▶ **Creamy Rice Cereal with Gingery Blueberries (page 63)**

▶ **1 cup herbal tea**

▶ **Basmati Rice Burgers with Pinto Beans (page 80)**

▶ **½ cup cooked carrots sprinkle with ¼ teaspoon cinnamon, ½ teaspoon lemon juice**

▶ **1 cup fresh arugula tossed with ½ cup sliced oranges, drizzled with balsamic glaze**

▶ **Fruit Kabobs with Peach Cream Dip (page 167)**

▶ **Tomatoes Stuffed with French Lentils (page 107)**

▶ **½ cup steamed brown rice**

▶ **1 cup torn romaine lettuce tossed with ¼ cup halved cherry tomatoes, ¼ cup sliced cucumber, ½ cup red pepper strips, drizzled with champagne vinegar**

DAY TWO

▶ **Vanilla French Toast (page 61)**

▶ **½ cup sliced fresh peaches**

▶ **Black Bean and Corn Salad with Lime (page 73)**

▶ **3 whole wheat breadsticks**

▶ **Field green salad tossed with ¼ cup diced zucchini, 1 small cubed tomato, ¼ cup shredded carrots**

▶ **1 medium apple**

▶ **Italian Chickpea Nibbles (page 169)**

▶ **Quinoa with Navy Beans and Almonds (page 109)**

▶ **½ cup steamed fresh broccoli florets mixed with ½ cup steamed cauliflower topped with 1 tablespoon vegan Parmesan cheese and ¼ teaspoon dried oregano**

▶ **1 small whole wheat roll**

▶ **½ cup fresh cut pineapple**

APPENDIX A
Quick & Easy Shopping List

FRESH HERBS:

Basil

Cilantro

Mint

Parsley

Rosemary

Sage

Thyme

DRIED HERBS:

Basil

Bay leaf

Oregano

Thyme

SPICES:

Black pepper

Cajun seasoning

Cardamom

Cayenne pepper

Chili powder

Chipotle powder

Cinnamon

Coriander (ground and seeds)

Cumin (ground and seeds)

Curry powder

Dried ancho chili

Dry mustard

Fennel seeds

Garlic powder

Ginger

Ground allspice

Nutmeg

Onion powder

Paprika (smoked, sweet)

Red pepper

Saffron

Turmeric

SEASONINGS:

Black bean sauce

Chili paste

Chutney

Enchilada sauce

Garlic bean sauce

Grand Marnier

Hot sauce

Ketchup

Liquid smoke

Low-sodium soy sauce

Mirin

Mustard (Dijon, stone-ground, whole-grain)

Salsa

Salt (kosher, sea salt)

Tahini

Tamari

Tomato paste

Vegan hoisin

Wine (red, rice, white, Marsala)

Worcestershire sauce

VINEGARS:

Apple cider

Balsamic

Red wine

Rice

Sherry

White wine

CANNED AND JARRED:

Artichoke hearts

Black beans

Black-eyed peas

Capers

Chickpeas

Chipotle chili peppers in adobe

Fava beans

Great northern beans

Green chiles

Olives (kalamata, black)

Orange juice

Pineapple

Pineapple juice

Pinto beans

Piquillo peppers

Pumpkin

Red kidney beans

Strawberries

Tomato juice

Tomatoes

White beans

FROZEN:

Cherries

Corn

Edamame

Fava beans

Green peas

Phyllo dough

PASTA:

Elbow macaroni

Fettuccine

Soba

Udon

whole wheat couscous

whole wheat pasta shells

whole wheat penne

whole wheat rotini

GRAINS:

Arborio rice

Barley

Brown Arborio rice

Brown basmati rice

Bulgur wheat

Cornmeal

Instant polenta

Lentils (red, yellow, green)

Oats

Popcorn kernels

Quick-cooking brown rice

Quinoa (regular, red)

Short-grain brown rice

Wild rice

SWEETENERS:

Agave nectar

Light brown sugar

Maple sugar

Sugar

DRIED FRUIT:

Apricots

Cranberries

Pitted dates

Raisins

BAKING:

   Active dry yeast

   All-purpose flour

   Almond extract

   Arrowroot

   Baking powder

   Baking soda

   Cooking spray

   Ener-G Egg Replacer

   Flaxseeds

   Nuts (almonds, walnuts, pine nuts, Brazil nuts)

   Nutritional yeast

   Olive oil

   Tortilla chips

   Unbleached white flour

   Vanilla extract

   whole wheat flour

   whole wheat pastry flour

BAKED GOODS:

   Bread crumbs (panko)

   Graham crackers

   Hamburger buns (whole wheat, multigrain)

   Italian baguettes

   Pumpernickel bagels

   Whole-grain bread

   whole wheat pita

   whole wheat tortillas

FRUITS AND VEGETABLES:

   Apples

   Arugula

   Asparagus

   Avocados

   Bananas

   Beets

   Bell peppers (green, orange, red, yellow)

   Blueberries

Broccoli

Cabbage (green, purple, savoy)

Carrots

Cauliflower

Celery

Chives

Corn

Cucumbers

Eggplant

Fennel

Garlic

Ginger

Grapes

Habanero chiles

Jalapeños

Jicama

Leeks

Lemons

Lemongrass

Lettuce

Limes

Mangoes

Mushrooms (porcini, cremini, button, portobello, shiitake, oyster)

Onions (white, red, yellow, green)

Oranges

Peaches

Potatoes

Pineapples

Poblano chiles

Raspberries

Shallots

Spinach

Sugar snap peas

Sweet potatoes

Tomatillos

Tomatoes

Yellow squash
Zucchini

REFRIGERATED ITEMS:
Almond milk
Cheddar-style soy cheese
Chocolate soy milk
Dairy-free sour cream
Light coconut milk
Miso
Rice cheese
Rice milk
Seitan
Soy creamer
Soy milk
Soy yogurt
Tempeh
Tofu
Vegan soy Parmesan cheese
Vegetarian bacon
Vegetarian sausage

EXTRA:
Vegetable broth

APPENDIX B
Convenience Foods

HERE ARE SOME convenience foods to keep on hand for a super-quick meal or snack.

BREAKFAST:
Instant oatmeal
Kashi 7 Whole Grain Cereals Puffs
Low-fat soy milk, rice milk, and almond milk
Silk Live! Soy Yogurt
Trader Joe's Organic High Fiber O's cereal
Trader Joe's Soy Yogurt
Trader Joe's Quick Cook Steel Cut Oats

LUNCH OR DINNER:
Amy's Light in Sodium Organic Traditional Refried Beans and
   Vegetarian Baked Beans
Amy's Non Dairy Vegetable Pot Pie
Amy's Roasted Vegetable Pizza
Boca Burgers Original Vegan
Canned chickpeas, drained and topped with seasoned rice
   vinegar
Edward & Sons Organic Miso-Cup Traditional Soup with Tofu
Fantastic Foods: http://www.fantasticfoods.com/
Food for Life Organic Sprouted Corn Tortillas

Gardein products (under the "It's All Good" label)

House Foods Tofu Shirataki Noodles: http://www.house-foods.com/

Imagine Soups: http://www.imaginefoods.com/

Kashi Black Bean Mango frozen dinner entrée: with black beans, plantains and mango: http://www.kashi.com/

Lightlife Smart Dogs

Olive Valley Falafel

Prepared vegan sushi (e.g., cucumber or avocado rolls)

Road's End Mac and Chreese

Sunshine Veggie Burgers: http://sunshineburger.com/index2.html

Thai Kitchen boxed noodles, with tofu and frozen veggies added

Thai Kitchen Rice Noodle Bowls (look for "Vegan" on the label) and Instant Rice Noodle Soup

Tofurky Italian-style Deli Slices

Trader Joe's frozen veggies and potatoes

Trader Joe's Garden Patch Veggie Soup

Trader Joe's Burritos and Enchiladas

Trader Joes "Chicken" Nuggets

WestSoy Italian-style baked tofu. Excellent on rice or salads.

Wildwood prepared flavored tofu

SNACKS:

Baba ganoush

Baby carrots

Clif Bars

Cucumbers

Dried fruit

Dry-roasted edamame

Fruits such as apples, clementines, bananas, etc.

Garden-fresh salsa

LÄRABARs

Laura's Wholesome Junk Food: http://lauraswholesomejunkfood.com/

Prepared hummus

Rice cakes

Tortilla chips

METRIC CONVERSIONS

THE RECIPES IN this book have not been tested with metric measurements, so some variations might occur.

Remember that the weight of dry ingredients varies according to the volume or density factor: 1 cup of flour weighs far less than 1 cup of sugar, and 1 tablespoon doesn't necessarily hold 3 teaspoons.

GENERAL FORMULA FOR METRIC CONVERSION
Ounces to grams ➡ ounces x 28.35 = grams
Grams to ounces ➡ grams x 0.035 = ounces
Pounds to grams ➡ pounds x 453.5 = grams
Pounds to kilograms ➡ pounds x 0.45 = kilograms
Cups to liters ➡ cups x 0.24 = liters
Fahrenheit to Celsius ➡ (°F − 32) x 5 ÷ 9 = °C
Celsius to Fahrenheit ➡ (°C x 9) ÷ 5 +32 = °F

VOLUME (DRY) MEASUREMENTS
¼ teaspoon = 1 milliliter
½ teaspoon = 2 milliliters
¾ teaspoon = 4 milliliters
1 teaspoon = 5 milliliters
1 tablespoon = 15 milliliters
¼ cup = 59 milliliters
⅓ cup = 79 milliliters
½ cup = 118 milliliters
⅔ cup = 158 milliliters
¾ cup = 177 milliliters
1 cup = 225 milliliters
4 cups or 1 quart = 1 liter
½ gallon = 2 liters
1 gallon = 4 liters

OVEN TEMPERATURE EQUIVALENTS,
FAHRENHEIT (F) AND CELSIUS (C)
100°F = 38°C
200°F = 95°C
250°F = 120°C
300°F = 150°C
350°F = 180°C
400°F = 205°C
450°F = 230° C

LINEAR MEASUREMENTS
½ in = 1.5 cm
1 inch = 2.5 cm
6 inches = 15 cm
8 inches = 20 cm
10 inches = 25 cm
12 inches = 30 cm
20 inches = 50 cm

VOLUME (LIQUID) MEASUREMENTS
1 teaspoon = ⅙ fluid ounce = 5 milliliters
1 tablespoon = ½ fluid ounce = 15 milliliters
2 tablespoons = 1 fluid ounce = 30 milliliters
¼ cup = 2 fluid ounces = 60 milliliters
⅓ cup = 2   fluid ounces = 79 milliliters
½ cup = 4 fluid ounces = 118 milliliters
1 cup or ½ pint = 8 fluid ounces = 250 milliliters
2 cups or 1 pint = 16 fluid ounces = 500 milliliters
4 cups or 1 quart = 32 fluid ounces = 1,000 milliliters
1 gallon = 4 liters

WEIGHT (MASS) MEASUREMENTS
1 ounce = 30 grams
2 ounces = 55 grams
3 ounces = 85 grams
4 ounces = ¼ pound = 125 grams
8 ounces = ½ pound = 240 grams
12 ounces = ¾ pound = 375 grams
16 ounces = 1 pound = 454 grams

ACKNOWLEDGMENTS

THERE ARE SO many people to thank for working with us on this book.

First, we thank Mary Ann Naples and Beth Shepard, both outstanding literary agents, for their many insights and support that were instrumental in making this book a reality. Our editor, Katie McHugh, at Da Capo Lifelong Books brought the book to life, and we are grateful for her vision and wonderful spirit. We are also indebted to Lara Comstock for her insightful copyediting.

Making food beautiful was the task of our food stylist extraordinaire, Bonnie Di Tomo, and Kathleen Ferry, our photographer. Playing dual roles of tester and developer, we thank Angie Lee, chef and culinary instructor for Sur La Table and graduate of L'Academie de Cuisine, Bethesda, MD, for her scrumptious dips and spreads. And special thanks to Olga and Anna Berman for their zesty pizzas. Olga, a culinary instructor and food blogger and Anna, graduate of the Culinary Institute of America and food writer, created wonderful pizzas and lent their help to many other recipes.

We also thank Laurie Wright, John Netzel, and Mary Ohno for sharing their yummy recipes with us. Our team of testers did it all with smiles and enthusiasm: Peggy Doerwaldt, Leah Koeppel, Susan Levin, Ruby Lathon, Debbi Miller, Sarah Murphy, Emily Richard, and Betsy Wason. Special hats-off to Amber Green, RD, for expertly handling the nutritional analysis and recipe formatting.

Finally, two people deserve special mention:

Chef Jason Wyrick is the executive chef of Devil Spice (www.devilspice.com), Arizona's only vegan catering company, and *The Vegan Culinary Experience*, the only vegan culinary magazine designed by professional chefs. Jason reversed his diabetes through a vegan diet and has helped innumerable people improve their health through delicious, healthy, compassionate cuisine. He provided several recipes that added immeasurably to this book. His passion for plant-based foods shines through every one.

Jill Eckart managed the entire testing team as well as many editorial aspects of this book, contributed delicious recipes of her own, and handled the entire process with skill, expertise, and good humor. This book would never have seen the light of day without Jill's outstanding work.

NEAL BARNARD, MD
ROBYN WEBB, MS

ABOUT THE AUTHORS

ABOUT NEAL D. BARNARD, MD

Neal Barnard, MD is a physician, clinical researcher, Adjunct Associate Professor of Medicine at the George Washington University School of Medicine, and principal investigator of a major study on diet and type 2 diabetes, funded by the National Institutes of Health. His research studies have demonstrated the surprising power of diet and lifestyle changes for people with diabetes, cholesterol problems, excess weight, menstrual pain, PMS, and other health problems.

Dr. Barnard's scientific articles have appeared in *Scientific American*, the *American Journal of Cardiology, Pediatrics*, the *American Journal of Clinical Nutrition*, the *Archives of Family Medicine*, the *Journal of the American Dietetic Association, Lancet Oncology*, the *Journal of Nutrition Education, Obstetrics & Gynecology, Nutrition Reviews*, the *American Journal of Medicine*, and *Preventive Medicine*, among other leading journals, and he is a reviewer for *The Lancet*, the *American Journal of Cardiology, Preventive Medicine, Appetite*, and the *European Journal of Clinical Nutrition*.

Dr. Barnard is president of the Physicians Committee for Responsible Medicine (PCRM), a nonprofit organization that conducts clinical research, promotes preventive medicine, particularly good nutrition, and tackles controversies in medicine and research. PCRM's Cancer Project provides nutritional help to cancer patients and their families. Dr. Barnard is also a Life

Member of the American Medical Association and a member of the American Diabetes Association.

ABOUT ROBYN WEBB

An award-winning nutritionist and nationally recognized cookbook author and spokesperson, Robyn Webb is a passionate advocate of cooking well and eating wisely. She is Food Editor of *Diabetes Forecast* magazine and a frequent contributor to *Cooking Light*. Through her longtime collaboration with the American Diabetes Association, Webb has published six cookbooks that stress the use of fresh ingredients to create naturally simple gourmet meals, including *Diabetic Meals in 30 Minutes or Less* and *The Diabetes Food and Cooking Bible*. Webb's recipes are also featured on www.Keebler.com and www.allrecipes.com.

Webb has taught thousands of people how to achieve good health while enjoying flavorful, fresh foods. For twelve years, Webb owned and operated A Pinch of Thyme Cooking School and currently teaches private lessons and corporate lectures on cooking and health. She is a recipient of the President's Council on Fitness' Healthy American Fitness Leader Award, an active member of the International Association of Culinary Professionals, and holds a Master's degree in nutrition from Florida State University.

Webb has been profiled by many media venues including CBS News with Dan Rather, Lifetime, The Food Network, and The Discovery Channel, among many others, and is the host of the Cable Ace award-winning broadcast Healthline on Washington's News 8. She lives in Alexandria, VA.

INDEX

Dr. Neal Barnard's Program for Reversing Diabetes (Barnard), 36

Edamame and Quinoa Salad, 76
Eggplant, Artichoke, Red Pepper, and Black Olive Pizza, 120
Eggplant Salad, 185
English cucumber, in Udon Noodle Salad, 72
entertaining, 173–174. *See also* menus
Esselstyn, Caldwell, 21
European Prospective Investigation into Cancer and Nutrition (EPIC), 19

fava beans, 160
    Bissara, 160
    Fava Bean and Tomato Stew, 79
fennel, fresh, 100
    Fennel and Tomato Salad, 190
    in Winter Vegetable Potage, 100
fennel seeds
    Fennel Vinaigrette, 190
    in Sweet Potatoes and Chickpeas in Chili Sauce, 112
Fettuccini with Roasted Peppers and Zucchini, 105
fiber, dietary, 32, 34–35, 39
Fire-Roasted Tomato Black Bean Chili, 99
Food for Life TV, 14
French Country Stew, 97
French fries, butternut squash as, 97
French Toast, Vanilla, 61
Frittata, Spicy Spinach, 58
frozen foods, 205
fruit, dried, 206
    in Fresh Strawberry Pie, 197
    in Moroccan-Style Pilaf, 136
fruit, fresh, 35, 57, 164, 179, 207–208
    Baked Apples in Phyllo Dough, 172
    Banana Cashew Cream, 197
    Banana-Ginger Pancakes, 57
    Chocolate Cherry Nirvana, 168
    Creamy Fruit Smoothie, 164

Fruit Kabobs with Peach Cream Dip, 167
Gingery Pear and Sweet Potato Soup, 77
Grilled Peaches with Sweet Balsamic Glaze, 179
Peachy Keen Smoothie, 69
Spicy Gala Apple, Chickpea, and Mango Chutney Soup, 88
See also berries; oranges and orange juice
Fusilli with Sun-Dried Tomatoes and Artichoke Hearts, Italian, 106

Gala Apple, Chickpea, and Mango Chutney Soup, Spicy, 88
garbanzo beans. *See* chickpeas
garlic, 95
Garlic Mushrooms, 183
Garlicky Pinto Bean and Pasta Bake, 139
ginger, 63
    Asian Broth with Mushrooms, Tofu, and Ginger, 113
    Banana-Ginger Pancakes, 57
    Creamy Rice Cereal with Gingery Blueberries, 63
    in Gala Apple, Chickpea, and Mango Chutney Soup, 88
    Ginger Tofu, 145
    Gingery Pear and Sweet Potato Soup, 77
    in Sweet and Sour Tofu, 152
    in Trinidadian Curried Cauliflower, Potatoes, and Peas, 133
    in Udon Noodle Salad, 72
glycemic index, 36–37
grains, 45–46, 206
    Mixed Vegetable Curry with Whole Wheat Couscous, 126
    Polenta with Zesty Mushroom Sauce, 128
    See also quinoa; rice
Green Chili and Oyster Mushroom Crepes, 55
green peas
    in Fava Bean and Tomato Stew, 79

in Mixed Vegetable Curry with Whole Wheat Couscous, 126
Saffron Risotto with Peas and Asparagus, 189
Sweet Potato and Green Pea Curry over Brown Rice, 142
Trinidadian Curried Cauliflower, Potatoes, and Peas, 133
in Vegetable Paella, 144

healthful diet, 12–13, 17–18. *See also* vegan diet
healthful diet research
    changing diet in patients, 23–25
    DASH study, 36
    food testing, 19–23
    overview, 17–18
    simple observations, 18–19
HealthySchoolLunches.org, 15
heart patients, 19–21, 23–24, 33–35
herbs and spices, 42–43, 81, 177, 203
    cinnamon, 37, 167
    Minty Black Bean, Jicama, and Cucumber Salad, 92
    Spiced Pumpkin Oatmeal, 65
    Whole Wheat Pasta with Zucchini and Herbs, 177
    See also basil, fresh; cilantro, fresh; saffron
hoisin sauce, 44, 196
Hopi Corn and Chili Stew, 78
hormones, 39
Hummus Pizza, 93
hypertension, 6–7, 22, 27, 33, 35–36

ingredients, 41–50, 203–209. *See also* stocking your kitchen
insulin-like growth factor (IGF-I), 39
iron, 13
Italian Beans and Greens, 125
Italian Chickpea Nibbles, 169
Italian Feast menu, 175–179
Italian Fusilli with Sun-Dried Tomatoes and Artichoke Hearts, 106